DYNAMIC CAPABILITIES

DYNAMIC CAPABILITIES:

LITERATURE REVIEW AND A FIRST STEP TO OPERATIONALIZE
DYNAMIC CAPABILITIES,
VALUE IMPLICATIONS OF DYNAMIC CAPABILITIES DUE TO THEIR APPLICATION IN
TERMS OF TIME,
AND
THE PREDICTION OF THE VALUE MAXIMIZING POINT IN TIME TO PERFORM
RESOURCE BASE MODIFICATIONS

INAUGURALDISSERTATION

zur Erlangung der Würde eines Doctor rerum oeconomicarum
der Wirtschafts- und Sozialwissenschaftlichen Fakultät der Universität Bern

Achim Althaus

Die Fakultät hat diese Arbeit am 24. Mai 2012 auf Antrag der beiden Gutachter
Prof. Dr. Artur Baldauf und Prof. Dr. Engelbert Dockner als Dissertation angenommen, ohne
damit zu den darin ausgesprochenen Auffassungen Stellung nehmen zu wollen.

Cuvillier Verlag, Göttingen 2012

Bibliografische Information der Deutschen Nationalbibliothek

Die Deutsche Nationalbibliothek verzeichnet diese Publikation in der Deutschen

Nationalbibliografie; detaillierte bibliografische Daten sind im Internet über

http://dnb.d-nb.deiabrufbar.

1. Aufl. - Göttingen: Cuvillier, 2012

Zugl.: Bern, Univ., Diss., 2012

978-3-95404-148-0

Acknowledgments

During my work as a Project Controller in Research & Development at SEW Eurodrive, I often discussed with colleagues the question why SEW Eurodrive had been so successful in the past and what this firm should do to maintain competitive advantage in the future.

Starting my doctorial program four years ago at the Department of Management and Entrepreneurship of the University of Bern, I got the opportunity to familiarize myself with the dynamic capability concept, which has been developed to answer this and other related questions from a research based perspective. However, the insights I have developed during my dissertation could not have been performed without help and support.

For this reason, I would like to thank my mentor, Prof. Artur Baldauf as well as Prof. Engelbert Dockner, director of the Department of Finance and Accounting, Vienna University of Economics and Business.

Prof. Baldauf has supported me patiently during the dissertation process, especially with regard to the literature research and the writing process. Furthermore, Prof. Baldauf allowed me room for personal development and encouraged me to gain insights into a plurality of research methods and streams. In addition, Prof. Baldauf enabled and supported the cooperation with Prof. Dockner.

Prof. Dockner introduced me to real options research and supported me to develop a mathematical model which permitted me to investigate research questions related to dynamic capability and ambidexterity research. To promote the development of my dissertation he made several visits to Bern and encouraged me to visit him at Vienna. Without exception, the constructive discussions we had, via phone, e-mail, or face to face were highly motivating.

Furthermore, I would like to thank Prof. Ulf Schiller and Prof. Jochen Bigus as well as Prof. Steven P. Brown, Prof. Gregory Dess, Prof. Tomas M. Hult, and Prof. Hans Mühlbacher for their support and contribution of excellent ideas. I also thank Tatiana Romanova, Silvan Blum and my mother Jutta Althaus for stylistic support.

A dissertation project is a long term process. I would like to thank Simone Sesboué, Anita Hunziker, Karin Tremp, Christian Bischof, and in particular fencing master Ryszard Marszalek for supporting discussions. For encouragements and advices I thank Katrin Schlesiger and Karlheinz Althaus.

Contents

List of Tables

List of Figures

List of Abbreviations & Notations

ANOVA Analysis of variance

cf. Compare

e.g. For instance

GBM Geometric Brownian Motion

PDE Partial Differential Equation

R&D Research and Development

With regard to chapter 3

A Placeholder

$\tilde{A}$ Placeholder

B Placeholder

$\tilde{B}$ Placeholder

$dW_i(t)$ Wiener increments

$E\{\cdot\}$ Operator for actuarial expectation

c_0 Intensity of capability employment

i Placeholder for x, y

IC Investment costs

q Extend of capability expansion

qIC Investment costs depending on capability expansion

r Risk less discount rate

SV Salvage value

t Time

$\tilde{V}$ Firm value (suboptimal application of dynamic capabilities in terms of time)

ΔV Difference of firm values

V_{DC_i} Value of dynamic capability i

V_{Max} Firm value (optimal application of dynamic capabilities in terms of time)

V_{RB} Firm value of the reference firm

x Capability

y Capability

α Intensity of capability employment

γ_r Solution of quadratic equation ($r = 1, 2$)

ε_r Solution of quadratic equation ($r = 1, 2$)

$\theta_i(t)$ Exogenously given price process related to capability i

θ_{i0} — Starting values of θ_i ($\theta_i(t=0)$)

$\bar{\theta}_i$ — Threshold level, trigger level

μ_i — Time-invariant drift rate of Geometric Brownian Motion

σ_i — Time-invariant volatility of Geometric Brownian Motion

τ_s — Optimally chosen point in time to change capabilities ($s=1,2$)

$\tilde{\tau}_s$ — Suboptimally chosen point in time to change capabilities ($s=1,2$)

With regard to chapter 4

A — Placeholder

B — Placeholder

c_i — Intensity of market exploitation

$dW_i(t)$ — Wiener increments

$E\{\cdot\}$ — Operator for actuarial expectation

$E\{T_i\}$ — Expected first passage time

i — Placeholder for x, y

IC — Investment costs

r — Risk less discount rate

SV — Salvage value

t — Time

T	First passage time
V	Discounted expected cash flow
x	Product sold in a declining market
y	Product sold in an emerging market
γ_r	Solution of quadratic equation $(r = 1, 2)$
ε	Solution of quadratic equation $(r = 1, 2)$
$\theta_i(t)$	Exogenously given cash flow process related to product i
θ_{i0}	Starting values of θ_i $(\theta_i(t = 0))$
$\bar{\theta}_i$	Threshold level, trigger level
μ_i	Time-invariant growth rate
σ_i	Time-invariant cash flow volatility
τ_1	Optimal point in time to enter an emerging market
τ_2	Optimal point in time to exit a declining market
Φ_i	Placeholder $(\Phi_x = \mu_x, \sigma_x, IC; \ \Phi_y = \mu_y, \sigma_y, SV)$

Chapter 1

Three Research Objectives:

An Overview

To maintain or to even enlarge competitive advantage it is essential for firms operating in changing environments to adapt their resource base configurations in a well thought out way to external shifts. Dynamic capabilities describe the firms' capacity to accomplish this aim. In my dissertation I pursue three research objectives with regard to dynamic capability research. In chapter 2, I introduce the reader into dynamic capability research, state that no dynamic capability concept exists to investigate empirically dynamic capabilities across industries argue, however, that such an investigation is possible, and outline a first step to do so. In chapter 3, I deal with my second research objective. Using a mathematical model I investigate the value implications of dynamic capabilities. In chapter 4, which comprises my third research objective, I outline a model to solve the fundamental problem to accomplish an optimal ratio of explorative and exploitative activities. Each of these chapters starts with an introduction including the relevant literature, a detailed description of the research objective, the academic and normative implications as well as a detailed description of how I approach each research objective. In the main part of each chapter I pursue the research objective. I conclude each chapter with a discussion of the results, limitations and future research avenues. This chapter serves the reader as a first overview of my research objectives. In the last chapter of my dissertation I provide a general summary.

The efficiency of resources and their intra- and interfirm development might be improved by 'ad hoc problem solving' (Winter 2003), or repetitive utilization (Helfat & Peteraf 2003). However, firms are at risk to be captured by resource configurations which were successful in the past, but - because of environmental shifts - are not able to satisfy present or future demands. In this case, the absence of flexibility, also described as 'structural inertia' might jeopardize the long-term survival of firms (Hannan & Freeman 1984, Burgelman 2002, Gilbert 2005, Lavie & Rosenkopf 2006).

Recognizing the importance of such dimensions as knowledge, time, and innovation to achieve and maintain competitiveness, in the 1990's researchers developed ideas which resulted in the dynamic capability approach (Cohen & Levinthal 1990, Teece & Pisano 1994, Teece, Pisano & Shuen 1997). Indeed, issues related to modifying/adapting a firm's strategic resource base and its capabilities to react to external influences to achieve competitive advantage became a dominant theme in strategy research (Cohen & Levinthal 1990, Grant 1996, Henderson & Cockburn 1994, Kogut & Zander 1992, Nelson 1991, Teece & Pisano 1994, Williamson 1991, Zander & Kogut 1995), and were integrated in Teece et al.'s (1997) comprehensive research contributions. Even though different definitions of dynamic capabilities have been developed in the past years, Teece et al.'s (1997, p. 516) early definition of dynamic capabilities as "the firm's ability to integrate, build, and reconfigure internal and external competences to address rapidly changing environments" summarizes comprehensively the basic notion of dynamic capabilities.

With regard to Teece et al.'s (1997) dynamic capability definition the main objective of researchers is, accordingly, to investigate how and under what influence factors a firm achieves a resource base configuration that is closest to the benefit maximizing configuration determined by internal and external conditions (Lavie 2006). In this context, Teece et al. (1997) describe the dynamic capabilities concept as an integrative approach based on different research streams such as organizational learning (Argyris & Schön 1978), as evolutionary theory (Nelson & Winter 1982), and as the resource-based view (Barney 1991). Beside the efforts of researchers to clarify the nature of dynamic capabilities in order to suggest a comprehensive definition (Helfat 1997, Teece et al. 1997, Eisenhardt & Martin 2000, Griffith & Harvey 2001, Lee, Lee & Rho 2002, Zollo & Winter 2002, Winter 2003), the dynamic capability research is concerned with a multitude of research aspects. For instance, scholars examine the shaping process of dynamic capabilities (Zollo & Winter 2002, Zahra, Sapienza & Davidsson 2006, Ethiraj, Kale, Krishnan & Singh 2005) or investigate the effectiveness of dynamic capabilities on performance (Henderson & Cockburn 1994, Teece et al. 1997, Eisenhardt & Martin 2000, Ni & Wan 2008). Another research aspect is to clarify the structure of dynamic capabilities including insights from related research streams (Grant 1996, Sitkin, Sutcliffe & Schroeder 1994, Harreld, O'Reilly & Tushman 2007, Zollo & Winter 2002, Adner & Helfat 2003, Zott 2003, Schreyögg & Kliesch-Eberl 2007, Teece 2007, Marsh & Stock 2006, Lavie 2006).

Going through the literature of dynamic capabilities, I identified three research objectives. The first reveals that - despite the massive body of research contributions - a generally accepted dynamic capability concept[1] is still missing that enables researchers

---

[1]In this dissertation, I use the terms 'framework' (a set of principles or ideas used as a basis for one's decisions, etc.), 'concept' (an idea or a principle relating to something abstract), 'approach' (a way of dealing with something, esp. a problem) as synonyms (Crowther 1995).

to investigate dynamic capabilities empirically. Likewise, there exist no empirical research contributions that investigate dynamic capabilities across industries.

The academic interest to investigate this research objective rests upon the assumption that the dynamic capability approach is most promising to reveal the long-term competitive advantage of firms (Teece 2007). Accordingly, the core of my first research aim is to moot *if* an industry-crossing investigation of dynamic capabilities is possible and then to discuss *how* an empirical, industry-crossing investigation of dynamic capabilities can be accomplished.

Besides this academic interest, the research issue has also normative implications. Against the background of increasing environmental uncertainties evoked by large innovation rates and global changes in firms' environments, top managers are forced to pay increasingly attention to the accurate adaptation of the firms' value generating resource base. Therefore, it is on behalf of firms' decision makers to provide and maintain well-functioning, effective, and risk reducing instruments to adapt a firm's resource base to its environment, but also to shape the business environment to the firm's advantage (Teece 2007). Based on an empirically validated concept which describes how firms survive in changing environments researchers are able to identify the essential and most influential factors or even to deduce the principles of how managers should behave to ensure the long-living of "their" firms with regard to continual or disruptive environmental shifts.

I go into this research objective in chapter 2, "Literature Review & a First Step to Operationalize Dynamic Capabilities". To avoid redundance and a too extended overview, furthermore, to ensure a smooth transition to the main part of this research contribution, and also to provide a more specific literature selection with regard to the considered research contribution I refer the reader to section 2.1, "Introduction to the First Research Objective". Here, I first show the miscellaneousness of dynamic capability research and then lead the reader to the research aim comprising its academic and normative implications. I provide a detailed description of how I accomplish my research aim, including among others the processes of literature review ensuring an inter-subjective selection.

A further central issue in dynamic capability research is to understand the interrelation of dynamic capabilities and firm performance, respectively firm value (Teece et al. 1997, Eisenhardt & Martin 2000, Winter 2003, Zott 2003, Zahra et al. 2006). Despite a plurality of research contributions, the research question if dynamic capabilities possess value similar to the firms' resource base which is responsible for generating the current firm performance - perhaps even in a "dormant" state - is still unanswered. Furthermore, if dynamic capabilities possess value there remains the questions which factors determine the value of dynamic capabilities. In particular, it is of interest if the timing of the dynamic capability application has an impact on the value of dynamic capabilities or even on the firm value.

Summarized, my second research objective is to analyze "The Value Implications of Dynamic Capability" which I do in chapter 3.

To tackle this research objective I use, similar to Kogut & Kulatilaka (2001) and Kyläheiko, Sandström & Virkkunen's (2002), insights from real option theory. I outline a mathematical model consisting of one firm possessing the options, and therefore, the dynamic capabilities to change its value generating resource base depending on environmental shifts. Assuming that the firm behaves value maximizing, it is crucial to determine the value maximizing point in time in order to apply its dynamic capabilities.

From the results of my model I see that the value of a firm is given by the sum of the present and future value generation of the existing resource base (resource-based view) *and* the firm's ability to adapt this resource base in a value maximizing way (dynamic capability research). Furthermore, I am able to identify several factors which influence the value of dynamic capabilities and recognize that all these value determining factors are externally given. In this context, the point in time to execute dynamic capabilities has an impact not only on the value of dynamic capabilities but also on firm value.

Besides the capacity of my model to deepen the academic understanding of dynamic capabilities, I am able to infer different normative implications. Likewise, the simulations I do may function as a first step to support managers to gain a better understanding of how different factors influence the value of dynamic capabilities and, accordingly, the value of firms. Rather, the results open the field to discuss cost issues of dynamic capabilities with regard to the aim of their application (Winter 2003).

Furthermore, linked with insights of different research contributions (Eisenhardt & Martin 2000, Adner & Helfat 2003, Winter 2003, Zahra et al. 2006, Teece 2007) my model seems to be suitable to explain the existence of management consultancies. Indeed, based on my deliberations I suggest that firms' decision makers are well advised to hone the contact to management consultancies in order to be supported at the appropriate point in time in case a resource base change should be necessary. This approach seems to be a way to keep the firm value high, while avoiding costs to develop highly sophisticated dynamic capabilities (Winter 2003).

Again, to avoid redundance and a too extended introduction with regard to the other research gaps also, to ensure a smooth transition towards the main part of this research contribution and to provide a more specific literature selection with regard to the considered research contribution I refer the reader to the section "Introduction to the Second Research Objective 3.1" . In this section, I introduce the reader to the relevant literature with regard to my second research objective, point out the research gap, summarize my approach to solve the problem of the research gap, and refer to the empirical and normative implications of my research results.

My third research objective deals with ambidextrous organizations. The basic notion of ambidextrous organizations is to ensure or even enlarge long-term competitive advantage by deploying exploitation and exploration simultaneously (Duncan 1976, March 1991, Tushman & O'Reilly 1996, O'Reilly & Tushman 2007). Simplified, exploitation means to ensure current competitive advantage through technology and product improvement. Exploration means to invest in the development of new technologies or products that are distinctive from the existent ones (March 1991).

Besides the integration of exploitation and exploration (Raisch & Birkinshaw 2008) "the basic problem confronting an organization is to engage in sufficient exploitation to ensure its current viability and, at the same time, devote enough energy to exploration to ensure its future viability" (March 1991, p. 105).

In other words, firms are challenged to find the optimal balance of exploitative and explorative activities. Since the extent and consequently the ratio of both activities are given by the degree of resource investments in exploitation and exploration, the firms' capacity to act in an ambidextrous way depends on the firms' ability to adapt its resource base with regard to external shifts (O'Reilly & Tushman 2007). According to this line of reasoning, to balancing of exploitative and explorative activities, for instance with regard to declining and emerging markets, must be considered as a specific dynamic capability.

This central challenge to balance the exploitative and explorative activities in an optimal way with regard to environmental shifts represents the link between ambidexterity and dynamic capability research. This challenge to firms is also the subject of my third research objective which I pursue in chapter 4, "Optimal Timing of Resource Adaptation".

To approach my third research objective I outline a formal model describing a firm selling a product in a declining market and at the same time possessing the option to enter an emerging market. To exploit the declining market as long as it is profitable the firm deploys exploitative activities. To maintain and hone the option to enter the emerging market the firm deploys explorative activities. Since it is the aim of firms to maximize long-term profit I choose the maximization of the firm's profit as target dimension.

The first challenge to firms' decision makers now is to *determine* the profit maximizing point in time when to discard the exploitative activities to the benefit of resources or a scrap value, as well as to determine the profit maximizing point in time when to discard the explorative activities respectively to transform these activities into exploitative activities. Since the development of the declining and emerging market is subject to uncertainty, real option theory comes forward to solve this problem.

However, to prepare the resource base adaptation and to avoid conflicts due to resource allocation and finally to ensure the optimal ratio of exploration and exploitation, it is of crucial interest to managers to predict the profit maximizing point in time to execute a resource base adaptation. Therefore, the second challenge to firms' decision makers is to *predict* the profit maximization of dynamic capabilities. Since my former model only provides the possibility to determine the profit maximizing point in time in real time, I develop a mathematical instrument to predict the value maximizing point in time to introduce a newly developed product into a prospering market and to withdraw an exploited product from a declining market.

This first overview of my third research objective shows the academic and normative implications of my approach: Apart from the potential of my model to close a central research gap in ambidextrous research, an appropriate adapted model could serve managers as an instrument to deduce the optimal balance of exploitative and explorative activities. Based on this information managers should be able to improve the allocation of resources with regard to the firm's short- long term aims.

Likewise to the first and second research objective I refer the reader to the section "Introduction to the Third Research Objective 4.1" where I provide a detailed introduction including the decisive literature, emphasizing the research objective, the academic and

normative implications of my research objective and how I approach it.

Chapter 2

First Research Objective: Literature Review & a First Step to Operationalize Dynamic Capabilities

One central focus of strategic management research is to identify the basis of competitive advantage. The resource-based view is one theory to explain the competitive advantage of firms. Simplified, a firm is able to maintain or enlarge its competitive advantage when possessing resources which are valuable, scarce, inimitable or non-substitutable. However, to avoid losing the competitive advantage in dynamic environments, it is a requisite for firms to ensure a permanent resource base modification with regard to internal and external changes. The dynamic capability research investigates how firms accomplish the adaptation of their resource bases in an efficient and well thought out way. In this chapter, focusing on basic research streams, definitions, and conceptual research contributions, I first introduce the reader to dynamic capability research. Reviewing empirical research contributions, I notice that they are often data-driven, industry limited, or rather show the existence of dynamic capabilities than to measure their nature or functionality. However, using insights from conceptual research contributions I argue, that the development of an instrument that captures the nature of dynamic capabilities across industries is possible, outline a first step to establish an industry-crossing dynamic capability construct, and discuss my results with regard to those of other authors.

2.1 Introduction to the First Research Objective

For firms operating in the private market sector, competitive advantage is of critical importance to survive. To explain the sources of competitive advantage, researchers have developed different theories (Teece et al. 1997), such as the 'stategic conflict' (e.g. Shapiro (1989)), the 'market-based view' (e.g. Porter (1980*b*)), or the 'resource-based view' (e.g. Barney (1991)). While the strategic conflict focuses on how to manipulate the firm's environment including competitors, the market-based view is outlined to estimate the attractiveness of markets. The resource-based view is intended to explain the competitive advantage of a firm at a defined state in comparison to its competitors. However, firms and firms' environments are subjects of change.

To explain the long-term success of firms operating in changing environments researchers have delineated the dynamic capability concept (Teece et al. 1997, Eisenhardt & Martin 2000, Adner & Helfat 2003, Zollo & Winter 2002, Zott 2003, Ethiraj et al. 2005, Lavie 2006, Zahra et al. 2006, Schreyögg & Kliesch-Eberl 2007, Teece 2007). Simplified the notion of this concept is that there exist firm inherent institutions - dynamic capabilities - that enable firms "to integrate, build, and reconfigure internal and external competences to address rapidly changing environments" (Teece et al. 1997, p. 516). The close link between the resource-based view and the dynamic capability concept is not only given because resources are still considered to be critical on account of the competitive advantage of firms (Eisenhardt & Martin 2000), but also because dynamic capabilities are assumed to be resources (Helfat, Finkelstein, Mitchell, Peteraf, Singh, Teece & Winter 2007).

Researchers undertake efforts to understand the nature, application and function of dynamic capabilities, the effectiveness of dynamic capabilities on firm performance, as well as on the key factors which might influence dynamic capabilities such as the firm's environment, the role of manager, cost issues, etc. (Teece et al. 1997, Eisenhardt & Martin 2000, Makadok 2001, King & Tucci 2002, Zollo & Winter 2002, Adner & Helfat 2003, Helfat & Peteraf 2003, Winter 2003, Lavie 2006, Teece 2007). Furthermore, the researches include an investigation of external factors such as velocity of market change (Eisenhardt & Martin 2000), internal factors, for instance the co-evolution of capabilities and dynamic capabilities (Zahra et al. 2006), learning and knowledge (Zollo & Winter 2002), adaptation (Jarzabkowski 2004), the role of management (Adner & Helfat 2003, Ambrosini & Bowman 2009), and decision making in different contexts (Makadok 2001, Lavie 2006, Kay 2010). Further issues are for instance strategic entrepreneurship (Uhlenbruck, Meyer & Hitt 2003) or the dynamic capabilities in the context of ambidexterity (O'Reilly & Tushman 2007).

The number of articles published with reference to dynamic capabilities especially in the recent two decades[1] can be explained due to the fact that at the current status of strategic research the dynamic capability approach is most promising to reveal the source of firms' long-term competitive advantages.

However, despite these research efforts or even because of this massive body of research contributions in the dynamic capability field a generally accepted concept of dynamic capabilities that can be applied across industries is still missing. The realization of such a model implies the closing of a central research gap in strategic management,

---

[1]Stefano, Peteraf & Verona (2010) assumes that since 2006 more than 100 articles per year with reference to dynamic capabilities have been published in business and management journals.

namely the exposure of long-term competitive advantage of firms operating in changing markets (Teece et al. 1997, Teece 2007).

However, to outline a model that can explain the long-term success of firms is one matter. Another is to find empirical evidence of the accuracy of such a model. Based on an empirically validated model that captures the key success factors of dynamic capabilities across industries, researchers could derive principles how firms should behave depending on internal and external factors. The normative implications of such principles is evident: managers would be able to execute resource base changes not only more efficiently and effectively but also at lower risk. In recent literature efforts have been made to develop such a model (Wang & Ahmed 2007, Ambrosini & Bowman 2009, Barreto 2010), however, they are established on or include critical issues that have to be discussed.

In this chapter, my research objectives are *a*) to introduce the reader into dynamic capability research, *b*) to demonstrate that there neither exists an industry-crossing empirical investigation of dynamic capabilities nor a comprehensive conceptual outline to operationalize dynamic capabilities, *c*), to argue on the basis of insights of conceptual research contributions that an industry-crossing operationalization of dynamic capabilities is possible, *d*) to outline a first step towards an operationalization of dynamic capabilities, and *e*) to discuss my approach in comparison to those of other researchers.

Accordingly, I follow Webster & Watson's (2002) proposition to conduct first a literature review and then to propose a conceptual model. More concrete, I first introduce the reader to the fundamental research streams on which the dynamic capability concept is based. Since definitions often facilitate the introduction and the understanding of specific, complex research areas, in the following I present a number of dynamic capability definitions and at the same time distinguish between dynamic capabilities and the value generating resource base. Furthermore, the investigation of dynamic capability definitions indicates that none of the different dynamic capability concepts is restricted to a specific industry sector.

This subsection is followed by an investigation of influential dynamic capability concepts. Here, as a further introduction into dynamic capability research, I focus on existing key research contributions and demonstrate the often complementary but also contradictory plurality of research contributions. One finding is that there exists no comprehensive concept that enables an empirical, industry-crossing investigation of dynamic capabilities. At the same time, the conceptual research contributions provide reasons to assume that an industry-crossing operationalization of dynamic capabilities is possible.

However, there might already exist industry-crossing empirical investigations of dynamic capabilities. Therefore, in the next section, I deal with the efforts of researchers to operationalize dynamic capabilities including their empirical investigations. I notice that these research contributions are often data-driven, or investigate a specific aspect, or rather go into the existence of dynamic capabilities but not their nature, and that common characters with regard to the research contributions hardly exist.

As there neither exist industry-crossing empirical research contributions nor comprehensive conceptual research contributions to operationalize dynamic capabilities, the logical consequence is to discuss *if* an industry-crossing operationalization of dynamic capabilities is possible and *how* this might be accomplished.

Since dynamic capabilities are closely linked to firm performance I close this section with an investigation of the relation of dynamic capabilities and firm performance.

In section 2.3, I use insights of conceptual and empirical research contributions, to argue that specific features or characteristics of dynamic capabilities should occur industry independently and thus outline my deliberations towards an operationalization of dynamic capabilities across industry boundaries.

In the last section of this chapter I recapitulate my research contributions, compare my approach to operationalize dynamic capabilities with those of other researchers, show limitations of my own model and then sketch future research possibilities.

The initial point of this dissertation in general, but in particular with regard to this chapter has been to search the database EBSCO for articles including the term dynamic capabilities. After a first analysis, of these articles, I dealt with articles that use dynamic capabilities as a central term. To ensure the inter-subjectiveness of my literature selection and analysis this process was accompanied by stimulating sessions of productive information exchange with PhD students working on this topic. A series of profound and serious discussions not only with PhD students but also with different Professors has served to make a balanced and deliberated selection of articles that not only contribute highly to my intended research objective but also ensure the inter-subjectiveness of my research. Finally, the key studies I used to accomplish my research objective have mainly been published in leading management journals such as Academy of Management Review, Administrative Science Quarterly, International Journal of Management Reviews, Journal of International Business Studies, Journal of Management, Journal of Product Innovation Management, Organization Science, and Strategic Management Journal.

Furthermore, Teece et al.'s (1997) article represents in so far a milestone in dynamic capability research as the authors compare the idea of dynamic capabilities with other theories which explain competitive advantages such as 'competitive forces' (Porter 1980*a*), 'strategic conflict' (Shapiro 1989), or the 'resource-based perspective' (Barney 1991). Teece et al.'s (1997) understanding of dynamic capabilities establishes the basis of scientific contributions meant to extend the dynamic capability knowledge. Therefore, although there exist research contributions linked to the 'dynamic capability' topic published before 1997 (cf. section 2.2.1), I in particular focus on concepts published after Teece et al.'s (1997) article.

In the meantime the inter-subjectiveness of my research selection has been confirmed by Stefano et al.'s (2010) research contribution. Applying co-citation analysis Stefano et al. (2010) identify four factors that describe the structure of the dynamic capability research contributions. The four factors are 'foundations and applications' (factor 1), 'interrelationship with other theoretical perspectives' (factor 2), 'issues of governance structure' (factor 3), and 'transformation processes and entrepreneurship' (factor 4). Regarding my research goal, factor 1 is decisive. This factor describes "the structural center of the dynamic capabilities domain" and comprises 29 of 40 articles Stefano et al. (2010) used for their analysis of various contributions, such as those of Teece et al. (1997), Eisenhardt & Martin (2000), Zollo & Winter (2002), Helfat (1997), Makadok (2001), and Winter (2003). 17 of 20 papers, the most cited of Stefano et al.'s (2010) panel, are considered by this factor. These 17 papers encompass 90,6% of the citation total in this research field. Therefore, Stefano et al. (2010) assume that these articles are foundational within the dynamic capabilities research field. The research object of these articles is to describe the dynamic capability construct, to understand the application as well as the effects of dynamic capabilities, and the processes through which dynamic capabilities are evolved and deployed (e.g. Helfat & Raubitschek (2000); Benner & Tushman (2003); Helfat & Peteraf (2003)). Articles loading on this factor deal with key issues of dynamic capabilities such as the role of managers supporting the creation, execution, and maintenance of dynamic capabilities (e.g. Makadok (2001); King & Tucci (2002); Adner & Helfat (2003)).

Out of the 29 articles concerning factor 1, I considered 9 articles with regard to my research aim to analyze the nature, the application, the evolution and development, the key issues of dynamic capabilities as well as the influencing factors of dynamic capabilities and their effectiveness, while not one of my selected articles can be found in factors 2, 3 or 4. Furthermore, I considered 6 of the 8 and 7 of the 11 most cited articles to achieve my research goal[2].

This result is less surprising, since Stefano et al.'s (2010) approach to select the appropriate research contributions with regard to their research goal, is similar to my

---

[2]With regard to articles published in Management Journals prior to 2008, available in the Thomson-ISI Web of Science database (Stefano et al. 2010)

approach or that of Barreto (2010). Here, I used 7 of the 9 articles Barreto (2010) considers as the main alternative conceptions with regard to dynamic capability research.

Of course, there are articles Stefano et al. (2010) and Barreto (2010) take into account that are not part of my selection. And yet, these authors do not consider articles such as Lavie (2006) (Barreto 2010, Stefano et al. 2010) or Schreyögg & Kliesch-Eberl (2007) (Stefano et al. 2010), whose research contributions I still recognize as remarkable.

2.2   Theoretical Foundations

The main research objective of this section is to introduce the reader into the dynamic capability research and to demonstrate that no conceptual approach exists that enables an industry independently investigation of dynamic capabilities. However, I will use insights of conceptual research contributions to *a*) demonstrate that an industry-crossing investigation of dynamic capabilities is possible and to *b*) provide a first step to do so. To accomplish these research objectives, I first identify the research streams on which dynamic capability research is based. I further analyze a number of dynamic capability definitions. This analysis indicates that scholars develop dynamic capability concepts industry independently. The following discussion of the main key findings of influential research contributions confirm this insight. Since researchers assume a(n) (indirect) link between dynamic capabilities and firm performance I conclude this part of my research contribution investigating the link between dynamic capabilities and firm performance.

2.2.1 Basic Research Streams

To get a better understanding of the contents of concepts, approaches, or frameworks, it is often advisable to clarify the origin, or the development of the research streams. In the case of dynamic capability research, scholars conceive their research area as an integrative approach of different research streams to explain wealth creation of firms in fast changing environments (Teece 2007). They apply specific knowledge from three relevant research streams:

The first research stream - the resource-based view - focuses on resources which firms control (Barney 1986, Dierickx & Cool 1989, Peteraf 1993), in contrast to theories investigating industry structures (Porter 1980a), or the strategic positioning (Shapiro 1989). The basic idea developed within the resource-based view is that a firm's performance (competitive advantage) is a function of the value, scarcity, imitability, and substitutability of the firm's resource bases. The competitive advantage based on resource differences arises due to lower costs, a distinctly higher quality or on product performance (Teece et al. 1997). However, the resource-based view has been criticized for several reasons, in particular because of its static nature, since it doesn't explain "how and why certain firms have competitive advantage in situations of rapid and unpredictable change" (Eisenhardt & Martin 2000, p.1106).

The second research stream - the evolutionary theory (Nelson & Winter 1982) - refers to the implications of a changing environment and their influence on firms. In this context, competitive advantage is assumed to be innovation-based (Nelson & Winter 1982), and emerges as a result of 'creative destruction' of existing competencies (Schumpeter 1934). Consequently, firms are forced to develop new products and resource base configurations. This requires firms to continually reconfigure and revise their capabilities. The firms' ability to respond to a changing environment partly depends on the firms' historical development and position (Nelson & Winter 1982).

The third research stream contributing to the dynamic capability framework is organizational learning as a basic premise to recognize the potential or necessity of feasible changes (Cohen & Levinthal 1990). Argyris & Schön (1978) were among the first to emphasize the importance of organizational learning to firms. Their model is based on the idea that organizational errors are detected and corrected by the modification of underlying norms, policies and objectives of the organization. Consequently, researchers in the dynamic capability field stress learning mechanisms with regard to resource base configurations. Zollo & Winter (2002), for instance, identify experience accumulation through learning by doing (Levitt & March 1988), knowledge articulation, and knowledge codification as important for the development of firms' resource bases.

The dynamic capability approach contains insights from at least three research streams are integrated. Similar to the resource-based view, its research focus is aimed at investigating firms' internal resources. Indeed, some authors argue that the dynamic capability approach represents an extension of the resource-based view by emphasizing specifically the dimension of time (Eisenhardt & Martin 2000). Since the evolution of a firm's resource configuration largely depends on environmental changes, researchers in the field of dynamic capability benefit from insights of the evolutionary theory. To recognize environmental shifts, to absorb information, and to execute an appropriate resource adaptation, insights of the organizational learning theory represent an essential fundament of dynamic capability research.

2.2.2   Zero-Level & Higher-Order Capabilities

In section 2.2.1, I used a general approach as a first step to introduce the reader into the dynamic capability research field. However, analyzing the central terms of a research topic offers another way to introduce the reader into a complex research area. With regard to the research objective which I pursue in this chapter, I further use the analysis of dynamic capability definitions as a first approach to understand the focus of dynamic capability research. Since the nature of an ability applied to accomplish change depends on the object of change (Zahra et al. 2006), I enhance the understanding of dynamic capabilities by an analysis of definitions used to describe the object of change.

In dynamic capability research, there exists a large disagreement regarding the use and understanding of the central terms. Different authors use different terms comprising different contents. With regard to dynamic capability research, scholars usually distinguish between two central constructs. One term is used to describe a meta-construct which reflects the characteristics of a firm's ability to change the characteristics of another construct. The second term is used to describe the firm's ability to generate value by the application of stable routines. In other words, the first construct is used to describe the 'tool' applied by firms to reconfigure the value generating base of a firm in a purposeful way, and the second construct is used to describe the value generating base itself (mostly described by capabilities, resource base, asset base, etc.).

To analyze the literature with reference to my research issue I follow Winter's (2003) neutral terminology to distinguish between these two constructs. Winter (2003) uses the term 'higher-order capabilities' with reference to the fundamental task of the first construct mentioned above, and the term 'zero-level capability' with reference to the fundamental task of the second construct mentioned above.

Zero-Level Capabilities

With regard to dynamic capability research the descriptions of the 'zero-level capabilities' (Winter 2003) comprise such terms as 'component competence' (Henderson & Cockburn 1994), 'organizational capability' (Helfat 1997), 'competencies' (Teece et al. 1997), 'existing capabilities' or 'resources' (Eisenhardt & Martin 2000), 'operating routines' (Zollo & Winter 2002) 'operation routines' (Adner & Helfat 2003), 'operational capabilities' (Blyler & Coff 2003), '(organizational) capabilities on zero-level' (Zott 2003), 'resource configuration' (Ethiraj et al. 2005), 'zero-order processes (functional competences)' (Marsh & Stock 2006), 'substantive capabilities' (Lavie 2006), or 'assets' (Teece 2007). Considering this number of different terminologies, ambiguities in their meaning seem to be likely. However, when looking closer at the characteristics of these definitions, one gets the impression that the terms introduced by different authors differ more than their substantive meaning.

For instance, Winter (2003, p. 991) defines a 'zero-level capability' as a "high-level routine (or collection of routine) that, together with its implementing input flows, confers upon an organization's management a set of decision options for producing significant outputs of a particular type". This definition is similar to Zahra et al.'s (2006, p. 921) definition of a substantive capability as a "set of abilities and resources that go into solving a problem or achieving an outcome", whereas Helfat & Peteraf (2003, p.999) define a capability as the "ability of an organization to perform a coordinated set of tasks, utilizing organizational resources, for the purpose of achieving a particular end result", which is close to Grant's (1996, p. 377) definition of a capability as the "firm's ability to perform repeatedly a productive task which relates either directly or indirectly to a firm's capacity for creating value through effecting the transformation of inputs into outputs", or Lavie's (2006, p. 153) notion that capabilities are competencies defined as "a capacity to integrate, combine, and deploy tangible and intangible resources through distinctive organizational processes in order to achieve desirable objectives". However, considering these definitions the reader realizes that the fundamental aim of the 'object of change' is to perform a specific output based on specific activities in a most efficient way.

In order to achieve a comprehensive understanding of zero-level capabilities, Helfat et al. (2007) define the firm's resource base as "tangible, intangible or human assets (or resources) as well as capabilities, which the organization owns, controls, or has access to on a preferential basis" (Helfat et al. 2007, p. 4).

Higher-Order Capabilities

Contrary to the description of the zero-level capabilities, the term 'dynamic capability' has gained general acceptance to describe 'higher-order capabilities'. The first important dynamic capability definition is given by Teece et al. (1997, p. 516) when they claim that dynamic capabilities are "the firm's ability to integrate, build, and reconfigure internal and external competencies to address rapidly changing environments". In contrast to Teece et al. (1997), Eisenhardt & Martin (2000, p. 1107) define dynamic capabilities as "the organizational and strategic routines by which firms achieve new resource configurations as markets emerge, collide, split, evolve, and die". This definition is similar to Zollo & Winter's (2002, p. 340). They emphasize the importance of experienced approaches with regard to the aim of effectiveness of dynamic capabilities by defining dynamic capability as a "learned and stable pattern of collective activity through which the organization systematically generates and modifies its operating routines in pursuit of improved effectiveness". Furthermore, Winter (2003, p. 991) describes dynamic capabilities as "those that operate to extend, modify or create ordinary (substantive) capabilities". The strategic importance of dynamic capabilities is considered by Teece's (2007, p. 1319) definition: "Dynamic capabilities can be harnessed to continuously create, extend, upgrade, protect, and keep relevant the enterprise's unique asset base".

Helfat et al. (2007, p. 4) developed a generally accepted definition describing dynamic capabilities as "the capacity of an organization to purposefully create, extend, or modify its resource base". Helfat et al.'s (2007) definition is consistent with Winter's (2003) line of reasoning that the notion of dynamic capabilities does neither include "ad hoc problem solving solutions", nor the modification of the resource base by luck, coincidence, or a resource base change simply by the application of capabilities (Helfat & Peteraf 2003). Accordingly, essential characteristics of dynamic capabilities are their disposability and their repeatable application in a systematical and purposeful way (Teece 2007, Zahra et al. 2006).

Based on the reviewed definitions of dynamic capabilities, I state that researchers consider dynamic capabilities as the capacity of firms (operating in a changing environment) to modify their resource base. However, I notice that none of these definitions focuses on a specific industry. The only restriction considered in dynamic capability definitions is the importance of dynamic capabilities for firms operating in (fast) changing environments. In other words, reviewing the definitions of dynamic capabilities formulated by different scholars I conclude that the notion of dynamic capabilities is not restricted to specific industries. This insight indicates that researchers pursue the development of dynamic capability concepts that are not industry specific.

2.2.3 Conceptual & Empirical Research Contributions

In section 2.2.2, I recapitulate a number of capability and dynamic capability definitions. For a further introduction of the reader into the dynamic capability research, I now review and analyze a number of selected research contributions. Furthermore, I use the insights of the next section to demonstrate that, in spite of efforts in recent literature (Wang & Ahmed 2007, Ambrosini & Bowman 2009, Barreto 2010), no appropriate dynamic capability concept exists to operationalize dynamic capabilities in an industry-crossing way (cf. section 2.2.3). Since there might already exist empirical industry-crossing investigations of dynamic capabilities, in section 2.2.3 I focus on empirical research contributions with regard to dynamic capabilities. Here I notice that the analyzed empirical dynamic capability models seem to be data-driven and, therefore, industry dependent. Even so, I am able to use insights of this section to argue that an across industries operationalization of dynamic capabilities is possible.

To achieve my research goals, I draw my attention mainly to the research focus namely the foundations of dynamic capabilities, the underlying models and their empirical realization, and the key findings the authors provide. I show their complementary characteristics and stress the contradicting elements.

An overview of the main articles I have used is provided in the tables 2.1, 2.2, and 2.3 with regard to the conceptual research contributions, and in the tables 2.4 and 2.5 with regard to the empirical research contributions. In the context of my research goal, it is essential to provide the reader with the research focus of each article. Therefore, in the tables I have chosen the column 'Research Focus', regardless if they contain conceptual or empirical research contributions. Furthermore, the key findings are central and of main interest to the reader. Consequently, I added the column 'Key Findings' to each table. Since one prerequisite of my research goal is to understand the foundations of dynamic capabilities that researchers assume, I have further chosen the column 'Basic View of Dynamic Capabilities' with regard to articles that focus largely on conceptual deliberations. Here, since the fundamental assumptions of authors are reflected by their definitions of dynamic capabilities, I use these definitions, if possible. However, in some cases the authors do not provide their own definitions, but refer to the definitions of other authors or refer to a description of their fundamental assumptions of dynamic capabilities. In these cases, I summarize the authors' "basic views of dynamic capabilities" in the according arrays of the tables.

With regard to empirical research contributions the link between the chosen research contributions and dynamic capability research is often not evident. Since this link is a crucial criterion for my selection of the empirical research contributions and, at the same time, often explains the authors central research aims, I decided to elaborate the link to dynamic capability research and to add these insights into a further column. To further introduce the reader into the characteristics of the chosen empirical research contributions, and also to show the industry dependency of the research contributions I add the column 'Data'.

Table 2.1: Literature overview of selected conceptual research contributions (1/3)

Author(s)	Research Focus	Basic View of Dynamic Capabilities	Key Findings
Teece et al. (1997)	Dynamic capabilities as a resource of sustainable competitive advantage.	Firm's ability to integrate, build, and reconfigure internal and external competences to address rapidly changing environments.	Concept of dynamic capabilities can be set at the same level as the concepts of resource-based or market-based view.
Eisenhardt & Martin (2000)	Definition of dynamic capabilities, their origin, and dependence on market dynamics.	Firm's processes used to match and even to create market change (specifically the processes to integrate, reconfigure, gain, and release resources). Thus, dynamic capabilities are the organizational and strategic routines by which firms achieve new resource configurations as markets emerge, collide, split, evolve, and die.	Nature of dynamic capabilities dependent on market velocity.
Makadok (2001)	Two possibilities of rent creation: resource-picking and capability-building. Research on relationship and interaction of these variables.	Dynamic capabilities are defined as a special type of resource, in particular an organizational embedded nontransferable firm-specific resource, whose purpose is to improve the productivity of the other resources possessed by the firm.	Resource-picking and capability-building as two instruments to change resource base. Firm's choice depends on expected value of resource adaptation and complements with regard to all other resources.
Zollo & Winter (2002)	Evolution of dynamic capabilities and influence of learning mechanisms on dynamic capabilities.	A dynamic capability is a learned and stable pattern of collective activity, through which the organization systematically generates and modifies its operating routines in pursuit of improved effectiveness.	Dynamic capabilities emerge through the ability of the enterprise to learn.
Adner & Helfat (2003)	Investigation of the consequences of different corporate managerial decisions on business performance. Outline of a dynamic managerial capability concept.	Managerial decisions influence the firm's resource base. Decisions depend on the interaction of 'managerial human capital', 'managerial social capital', and 'managerial cognition'.	Faced with the same external environment, managers make different decisions which result in a heterogeneity of business performances. To explain this result Adner & Helfat (2003) outline the concept of dynamic managerial capabilities.
Helfat & Peteraf (2003)	Founding, development, and maturity of dynamic capabilities. Heterogeneity of organizational capabilities.	Definition according to Teece et al. (1997). Notation of the six R: retirement, retrenchment, renewal, replication, redeployment, recombination (phases of the capability lifecycle).	Capability-life-cycle-approach explains the diversity of firms.

Table 2.2: Literature overview of selected conceptual research contributions (2/3)

Author(s)	Research Focus	Basic View of Dynamic Capabilities	Key Findings
Winter (2003)	Definition of dynamic capabilities, distinction of different terms in literature.	Dynamic capabilities are those capabilities that operate to extend, modify, or create ordinary capabilities.	Confusion about types and benefits of dynamic capabilities arises from a too narrow view of the concept.
Blyler & Coff (2003)	Social capital as a part of dynamic capability. Relationship between social capital and rent appropriation patterns.	Definition according to Eisenhardt & Martin (2000): to acquire, integrate, recombine and release resources.	Explicit connection between social capital and dynamic capabilities. Social capital influences the distribution of rents.
Zott (2003)	Game-theoretical simulation of the relationship between dynamic capabilities and the emergence of intra-industry differential firm performance.	No own definition, but emphasis, that dynamic capabilities are the ability to generate alternative resource configurations by imitation and experimentation.	Time, costs and the ability of learning affect the enterprise performance. Even small varieties of these variables can lead to significant differences in performance.
Lavie (2006)	Reconfiguration mechanisms of capabilities of incumbents.	Dynamic capabilities can be seen as learned patterns of organizational activities providing a systematic means of modifying capabilities and operational routines.	Beside dynamic capabilities, other mechanisms to execute resource base reconfigurations exist (e.g. substitution, transformation, evolution).
Zahra et al. (2006)	(1) Interdependence of substantive and dynamic capabilities; (2) Role of organizational knowledge and skills; (3) Effects of organizational age/experience on the use of dynamic capabilities.	Clear distinction of dynamic capabilities and substantive capabilities. Indeed, dynamic capabilities influence substantive capabilities. However, to ensure efficiency dynamic capabilities must be adapted to substantive capabilities.	Evolution of dynamic capabilities and substantive capabilities are interdependent. Firm age/experience has an effect on dynamic capability characteristics.
Schreyögg & Kliesch-Eberl (2007)	Contradictions of existing dynamic capability models. Integration of dynamic dimensions into a concept of organizational capability.	Instead of dynamizing the capability conception, capability evolvement and system dynamization are conceived as two separate countervailing processes, which are performed simultaneously.	Existence of two balancing processes: organizational capabilities and a surveying process. If necessary, the second process initiates an alteration on the first process.
Teece (2007)	Nature and microfoundations of dynamic capabilities.	Teece (2007) disaggregates dynamic capabilities into the capacities sensing, seizing, and reconfiguration/transformation.	The survival of firms operating in fast changing environments depends largely on the existence of well functioning dynamic capabilities.

Table 2.3: Literature overview of selected conceptual research contributions (3/3)

Author(s)	Research Focus	Basic View of Dynamic Capabilities	Key Findings
Wang & Ahmed (2007)	Based on a clarification of the concept of dynamic capabilities, the authors identify the factors which reflect common features of dynamic capabilities. They integrate the antecedents and consequences into a model explaining firm performance.	Dynamic capabilities are a firm's behavioural orientation constantly to integrate, reconfigure, renew and recreate its resources and capabilities, and most important, upgrade and reconstruct its core capabilities in response to the changing environment to attain and sustain competitive advantage.	1. Market dynamism influences the development of dynamic capabilities; 2. Highly developed dynamic capabilities lead to particular capabilities driven by business strategy; 3. Dynamic capabilities and firm performance are mediated by capability development.
Ambrosini & Bowman (2009)	Review and synthesis of literature; identification of variables and processes that shape/create dynamic capabilities; outline of a model that explains competitive advantage including internal and external factors.	Dynamic capabilities are organizational processes in the most general sense, and their role is to change the firm's resource base. They are built rather than bought in the market, are path dependent and are embedded in the firm.	Characteristics of dynamic capabilities are shaped by market change, cost issues, time duration between application, role of managers, positions and paths. The value creation process of a firm (including dynamic capabilities) and the link between the outcomes is influenced by internal and external factors.
Katkalo, Pitelis & Teece (2010)	Clarification of definitions/charcteristics of resources/competences and dynamic capabilities.	Definition of Teece et al. (1997). Examples of dynamic capabilities can be product development (change routines), investment choices (analysis) or pioneering new markets (creative managerial and entrepreneurial acts)	Classification of dynamic capabilities according to their task in sensing, seizing, transforming. Because of the absence of a perfect environment, managers are asked to manage the different types of dynamic capabilities.
Barreto (2010)	Review of different dynamic capabilities research streams, identification of research gaps and limitions. Conceptualization of dynamic capabilities as an aggregated multidimensional construct.	A dynamic capability is the firm's potential to systematically solve problems, formed by its propensity to [1] sense opportunities and threats, [2] to make timely and [3] market-oriented decisions, [4]and to change its resource base.	Dynamic capabilities can be reflected by the four dimensions ([1]-[4]) listed in the definition. Discussion of the construct with regard to measurement, and consequences (firm performance). Development of theory boundaries (environmental conditions, types of firms)

Table 2.4: Literature overview of selected empirical research contributions (1/2)

Author(s)	Research Focus	Link to Dynamic Capabilities Research	Data	Key Findings
Henderson & Cockburn (1994)	Architectural competence & research productivity in pharma industries.	'Architectural competence': Ability of knowledge integration. 'Component competence': Possession of skills and assets specificity to particular local activities within the firm ⇒ 'Architectural competence' ≈ 'Dynamic capabilities'	Quantitative Data: n=3210 (1975-1988) Qualitative Data: a) primary data: textbooks, articles, etc., narrative stories; b) secondary data: firm level: n=120.	Architectural competence as a source of competitive advantage in research productivity.
Zander & Kogut (1995)	Codification and processing of knowledge. Transfer of capabilities.	Emphasis on the importance of re-combining the knowledge of the firm to enhance innovation. This ability is a 'distinctive capability'.	44 innovations of 20 firms; n=35	Median transfer time is five years. Despite the fact that all innovations in the study were protected, approximately two-thirds were imitated.
Helfat (1997)	Stocks of complementary know-how in organizations.	Dynamic capabilities enable firms to create new products and processes, and to respond to changing market conditions.	26 firms, n=156 (1976-1981)	No evidence of complementary know-how between 'firm-wide R&D capabilities' and 'coal conversion R&D'.
Griffith & Harvey (2001)	Integration of resource-based and market-based views on a global level.	Global dynamic capabilities are the creation of difficult-to-imitate combinations of resources, including effective coordination of inter-organizational relationships on a global basis that can provide competitive advantage to a firm.	250/52 Canadian, 250/36 Chilean, 100/20 British, and 100/22 (mailed/usable) Philippine distributors;	Effective implementing global dynamic capabilities is contingent on the degree of firm's power, derived from its internal (resource-based) and external (market-based) assets.

n= number of used samples.

Table 2.5: Literature overview of selected empirical research contributions (2/2)

Author(s)	Research Focus	Link to Dynamic Capabilities Research	Data	Key Findings
King & Tucci (2002)	Development of capabilities in enterprises to survive in quickly changing markets.	Definition according to Eisenhardt & Martin (2000), Teece et al. (1997), etc.	208 business units out of 174 firms (1976-1995)	Static experience (production & sales experience) is a good prediction of market entry. With deeper experience in existing markets, the possibility of entering a new market niche increases.
Adner & Helfat (2003)	Time-varying corporate effects associated with corporate-level managerial decisions. Concept of dynamic managerial capabilities.	Concept of "dynamic managerial capabilities": capabilities largely influenced by managers to build, integrate and reconfigure organizational resources and competencies.	Quantitative Data: 30 companies over a 21 - year time period; Qualitative Data: Wall Street Journal; Financial Reporting System	Heterogenous managerial decisions affect the variance of enterprise performance.
Ethiraj et al. (2005)	Managerial effort to build capabilities. Relationship of capabilities and firm performance.	Project management capabilities: acquired through deliberate and persistent investments in infrastructure and systems to improve the firm's software development process.	n=138 (1996-2001)	Capability improvement by investment or utilization contribute positively to project performance.
Marsh & Stock (2006)	Process of knowledge integration.	Demands require sustained innovation and development of a dynamic capability that enables a firm to create and reconfigure resources to adapt to changes in the competitive environment.	n= 79	Knowledge retention and interpretation activities contribute to the ability to apply prior developed knowledge. Formal audits, memos, and presentations are important contributions to effective retention and application of knowledge.

n= number of used samples.

Conceptual Research Contributions

Since Schreyögg & Kliesch-Eberl (2007) have already provided a review, discussion, and classification of the main important dynamic capability concepts (Teece et al. 1997, Eisenhardt & Martin 2000, Zollo & Winter 2002), I begin this section with their research contribution. Even though parts of Adner & Helfat's (2003) article contain empirical explorations, I discuss their research contributions in this context, since they provide a further interesting perspective to explain the reconfiguration process of the firms' resource bases. After presenting Schreyögg & Kliesch-Eberl's (2007) dynamic capability concept, I analyze the frameworks of Zahra et al. (2006), Helfat & Peteraf (2003), Winter (2003), Lavie (2006), Makadok (2001), Zott (2003), and Teece (2007).

Schreyögg & Kliesch-Eberl (2007) identify three important research streams within the dynamic capability research field. The first, the 'integrative approach' is based on Teece et al.'s (1997) idea that dynamic capabilities mechanisms are attributed to adaptation, integration, and reconfiguration, and determined by the firms' positions, paths, and processes. They assume that the long-term success of firms operating in environments of rapid technology change depends largely on the appropriate adaptation of internal technological, managerial, and organizational processes. According to Teece et al. (1997), dynamic capabilities obtain their strategic character because of their inimitability, or the incapability of markets to provide appropriate dynamic capabilities in terms of time, costs, and quality.

The second approach emphasized by Schreyögg & Kliesch-Eberl (2007), the 'radical dynamization approach', goes back to Eisenhardt & Martin's (2000) understanding of dynamic capabilities. Eisenhardt & Martin (2000) argue that dynamic capabilities are processes based on 'best practice', and, therefore, possess common features across firms. Consequently, in contrast to Teece et al.'s (1997) view, dynamic capabilities are only path dependent in their specific characteristics. Additionally, Eisenhardt & Martin (2000) claim that firms develop different dynamic capabilities depending on the markets they are operating in. In moderately dynamic markets, dynamic capabilities can be described as "detailed, stable processes with predictable outcomes", contrary to high velocity markets where dynamic capabilities are characterized by "simple, highly experiential and fragile processes with unpredictable outcomes" (Eisenhardt & Martin 2000, p.1105).

The third approach discussed by Schreyögg & Kliesch-Eberl (2007) is called 'innovation routines'. It is based on Zollo & Winter's (2002) research contribution and examines in particular the development of dynamic capabilities from the learning point of view. Zollo & Winter (2002) identify 'experience accumulation', 'knowledge articulation', and 'knowledge codification' processes as important when supporting the evolution of dynamic capabilities, but also when developing operational capabilities or routines.

Despite these obvious differences, there are some similarities between the approaches. In accordance with the resource-based view, and similar to Teece et al. (1997), Eisenhardt & Martin (2000) and Zott (2003) consider dynamic capabilities as firm inherent processes. The essence is, that these equifinal[3] (Eisenhardt & Martin 2000) or hard to identify (Teece

---

[3]Equifinality of dynamic capabilities: the development of dynamic capabilities start from different points and take unique paths. Due to 'best practice' deliberations, the resulting capabilities are similar in terms of key attributes (Eisenhardt & Martin 2000, p.1109).

et al. 1997) processes provide competitive advantage by enabling firms to respond quickly and adequately to changes concerning their environment. Zollo & Winter (2002) follow this argumentation, assuming that dynamic capabilities actuate effectiveness, because they consist of stable patterns, enabling firms to generate and modify operating routines systematically. The structure of these patterns is formed by experience and learning. This has been stressed in particular by Teece et al. (1997), Helfat et al. (2007), and by Adner & Helfat (2003).

In contrast to Teece et al. (1997), Eisenhardt & Martin (2000), and Zollo & Winter (2002), Adner & Helfat (2003) emphasize in their concepts of 'dynamic managerial capabilities' the role of managers. They argue, that managers operating in similar environments make different decisions because of heterogenous skills, education and working background (managerial human capital), social relationships (managerial social capital) and different perceptions, beliefs and decision making habits (managerial cognitions). The results of differences in managers' decision making are reflected in differences between firms' resource bases.

Based on the insights obtained by the examination of these research streams, Schreyögg & Kliesch-Eberl (2007) suggest a further dynamic capability concept and introduce the notion of 'capability monitoring', a function different from the operational level. The monitoring capability constitutes the link between the operational level and the internal, respectively external environment. Despite of the interrelatedness, the two countervailing systems function independently in terms of time and space and enable firms to make a clear distinction between value producing processes and processes enabling changes. Capability monitoring rather analyzes the internal and external environment and functions, therefore, as a proctection mechanism on the operational level. Consequently, the concept makes it possible to examine the evolution of capabilities and to avoid an integration of dynamics into capabilities.

In contrast to Schreyögg & Kliesch-Eberl (2007), Zahra et al. (2006) emphasize the interdependence of 'dynamic capabilities' and 'substantive capabilities'. According to Zahra et al. (2006), the characteristics of dynamic capability are highly affected by the nature of substantive capabilities, while the shape of substantive capabilities is the result of the application of dynamic capabilities. Considered from a time perspective, to ensure an increase of effectiveness and efficiency of dynamic and substantive capabilities, the further development of both is based on interwoven, complex, and intricate relationships. Zahra et al. (2006) assume that this relationship is moderated by firms' organizational knowledge and skills.

Unlike researchers mentioned before, Helfat & Peteraf (2003) argue that change and adaptation of 'organizational capabilities' can take place, to a certain degree, without the application of dynamic capabilities as intermediaries between capability improvement and firm performance. They outline a dynamic resource-based view - the 'capability lifecycle' - to explain firms' heterogeneity of organizational capabilities without the existence of dynamic capabilities. Helfat & Peteraf (2003) assume that, followed by the 'founding' and 'development' stage, after or even before the 'maturity stage', every capability passes at least through the 'retirement' (death), 'retrenchment', 'renewal', 'replication', 'redeployment', or 'recombination' stage. Consequently, the evolution of capabilities depends on historical antecedents in the form of previous capability evolutions which might result in the heterogeneity of firms' resource bases.

Similar to Helfat & Peteraf (2003), Winter (2003) introduces the notion of 'ad hoc problem solving' and considers the possibility of capability modification without the existence of dynamic capabilities. In contrast to the application of dynamic capabilities, ad hoc problem solving is not a repetitious process based on experience, or specific patterns. In fact, ad hoc problem solving is typically applied as an immediate response to unknown, unpredictable challenges arising from environment changes. Therefore, unlike to the development, maintenance, and application of dynamic capabilities to modify firms' resource bases, costs only emerge at the moment of the application of ad hoc problem solving. Consequently, depending on the quality and the long-term demand of resource adaptation, the development and maintenance of highly sophisticated dynamic capabilities might become disadvantageous to firms.

A more complex system to demonstrate different, however, planned possibilities of resource modification has been developed by Lavie (2006). Contrary to Eisenhardt & Martin (2000) who examine the influence of change velocity of markets on the nature of dynamic capabilities (Eisenhardt & Martin 2000), Lavie (2006) assumes that the choice of capability reconfiguration depends on the kind of technological change an incumbent is confronted with (external factor), as well as on the characteristics of the capabilities of change (internal factor).

Similar to Lavie (2006), Makadok (2001) assumes that a firm possesses the possibilities of 'resource-picking' and 'capability-building' to change its resource capacity in order to maximize economic rents. Based on these assumptions Makadok (2001) outlines a mathematical model to investigate the interaction between these distinct mechanisms. Makadok's (2001) results show that depending on the assumed circumstances, in some cases rent maximization is achieved by the exclusion of one of the mechanisms, in others by the complementary application of both mechanisms.

Another mathematical model has been developed by Zott (2003) who investigates how differences in firm performance within an industry might be linked to specific sub-processes of dynamic capabilities. To approach this research question, Zott (2003) assumes that dynamic capabilities influence firm performance indirectly by modifying 'competencies', 'operational routines', or 'resource positions'. Zott (2003), then, subdivides dynamic capabilities into the processes of 'variation', 'selection', and 'retention'. Each of these processes is linked to the specific influence factors 'costs', 'learning', and 'timing'. Using simulations, Zott (2003) is able to demonstrate that even minor initial differences among firms with regard to these influence factors might generate significant intra-industry differential firm performances.

Based on previous research contributions, the most comprehensive and most specific approach delivering detailed and practical information is Teece's (2007) description and analysis of the complex structure of dynamic capabilities. Similar to Zott (2003), Teece

(2007) identifies the processes 'sensing', 'seizing', and 'reconfiguring', which enable firms to deploy, create, and protect their assets which ensure the firms' long-term survival. The efficient functionality of these capacities rests upon distinct processes, procedures, organizational structures, decision rules, and disciplines, the 'microfoundations' of dynamic capabilities. In comparison to previous researchers, who rather consider dynamic capabilities as a 'black box', Teece (2007) aims at analyzing, unraveling, and demonstrating the nature of dynamic capabilities, especially by linking theoretical deliberations to practical observations.

In recent dynamic capability literature, I notice a research trend to outline concepts based on the insights of the literature reviews in order to operationalize dynamic capabilities (Wang & Ahmed 2007, Ambrosini & Bowman 2009, Barreto 2010). The approaches the authors choose are similar: For instance, Wang & Ahmed (2007) start with an extended investigation of the resource-based view, dynamic capabilities and the link to each other. The investigation includes a distinction of 'resources', 'capabilities' and 'core capabilities' as well as 'dynamic capabilities'. Ambrosini & Bowman (2009) provide an overview of the dynamic capability perspective, followed by a repetition of main the dynamic capability definitions. Similar to Wang & Ahmed (2007), Ambrosini & Bowman (2009) identify different categories of capabilities. Barreto (2010) analyzes dynamic capability research contributions with regard to the main definitions, the nature, the specific role, the relevant context, creation and development mechanisms, the outcomes, and the purpose of dynamic capabilities.

However, with regard to the authors' and my research contributions, more interesting are the outlined models the authors present. Here, Wang & Ahmed (2007) identify three main component factors of dynamic capabilities, which are 'adaptive capability','absorptive capability', and 'innovative capability'. Wang & Ahmed (2007) state that these component factors are embedded in firm specific processes. The dimensions of Barreto's (2010) dynamic capability construct are the firm's ability to ' (1) sense opportunities and threats', ' (2) to make timely and (3) market-orientated decisions', and to '(4) change its resource base'. Barreto (2010) emphasizes that his construct is formed by the four dimensions. Consequently, one dimension cannot represent the whole construct. Rather, the effectiveness and efficiency of the dynamic capability construct depends largely on the inter-play of the different dimensions. In contrast to Barreto (2010) and Wang & Ahmed (2007), Ambrosini & Bowman (2009) do not use distinctive component factors or dimensions to describe dynamic capabilities. They rather describe the nature of dynamic capabilities by "internal and external enablers and inhibitors of dynamic capabilities" (Ambrosini & Bowman 2009, p. 39). These are for instance the role of managers, social ties of individuals, leadership, and trust.

With dynamic capabilities as the central element, Wang & Ahmed (2007), Ambrosini & Bowman (2009) and Barreto (2010) outline different but similar models. All authors consider the firm's external environment as one element. Even so, the authors assume that dynamic capabilities have a significant influence on the long-term competitive advantage of firms. Here, Wang & Ahmed (2007) and Ambrosini & Bowman (2009) propose an indirect link between dynamic capabilities and firm performance, mediated by the resource base (Wang & Ahmed 2007) or the development of capabilities (Ambrosini & Bowman 2009), while Barreto (2010) ponders between different possibilities he found in literature. To summarize, even though the research focus as well as the approaches of Wang & Ahmed (2007), Ambrosini & Bowman (2009), and Barreto (2010) are similar, the main distinction of of these research contributions is - as shown above - the description of dynamic capabilities.

A further recent research contribution with the aim to consolidate dynamic capability research is that of Katkalo et al. (2010). They also discuss the notions of resources/competences and dynamic capabilities. According to the authors, dynamic capabilities can be classified as 'sensing', 'seizing', and 'transforming'. Similar to Barreto (2010), Katkalo et al. (2010) assume that, because of the the complexity of the firms' environments, a pure application of one of these capabilities is not plausible. Rather, the entrepreneurial skills of managers are asked to bundle and manage different types of dynamic capabilities.

Based on the above literature review, I introduce the reader into dynamic capabilities research and, at the same time, demonstrate the plurality of research aspects. In spite of recent research contributions (Wang & Ahmed 2007, Ambrosini & Bowman 2009, Barreto 2010), I use the insights of this section to argue in section 2.3 that no conceptual dynamic capability framework exists that allows the realization of an instrument that is able to investigate empirically the nature of dynamic capabilities across industry boundaries. Since there might already exist empirical research contributions that provide appropriate models to investigate dynamic capabilities across industry boundaries, I now focus my attention on empirical research contributions.

Empirical Research Contributions

In the following section, I focus attention on empirical efforts with regard to dynamic capability research. Within the range of my research objectives the only research aim of this section is to demonstrate that empirical research contributions with regard to dynamic capabilities provide insights into rather specific aspects of dynamic capabilities and often seem to be data-driven. To achieve this research aim and at the same time to show the inventiveness of the different scholars as well as the investigated characteristics of dynamic capabilities it is most expedient to review the selected research contributions as an orientation in terms of their research focuses, the link to dynamic capability research, the used data, and of course their key findings.

My research efforts confirm Ambrosini & Bowman's (2009) and Pablo, T. & Casebeer's (2007) results that only few empirical research contributions exist that refer to dynamic capabilities. The journals in which the discussed articles are published (Journal of International Business Studies, Management Science, Organization Science, Strategic Management Journal, The Journal of Product Innovation Management) ensure their scientific impact. The tables 2.4 and 2.5, summarize the following examination by using the dimensions mentioned above.

Henderson & Cockburn (1994) explore the role of 'architectural competence' and 'component competence' on the basis of pharmaceutical research productivity. Integrating Henderson & Cockburn's (1994) research contribution into the dynamic capability research stream, the capability 'architectural competence' corresponds with dynamic capabilities (higher-order capability), and 'component competence' with capabilities (zero-level capabilities). While Henderson & Cockburn (1994) investigate the functionality of dynamic capabilities in terms of external knowledge integration, the centre of Zander & Kogut's (1995) research contribution is the resource reconfiguration due to capability transfer. More concrete, Zander & Kogut (1995) investigate the speed of capability transfer across firm boundaries depending on the degree of codification as well as on the difficulty to transfer capabilities.

A more firm internal orientated model is outlined by Marsh & Stock (2006). They assume that processes, such as 'growth', 'adaptation', and 'renewal', can take place more efficiently and rapidly through sophisticated 'intertemporal knowledge integration'. Marsh & Stock's (2006) model is based on the assumption that new product development performance is directly influenced by 'intertemporal integration' of knowledge, 'knowledge retention', and 'knowledge interpretation', whereas 'knowledge integration' is simultaneously influenced by 'knowledge retention' and 'knowledge interpretation'. The importance of knowledge to influence the shaping process of capabilities is also central to Ethiraj et al.'s (2005) research focus. Ethiraj et al. (2005, p.33, 34) assume that first, the project performance increases due to the development of client specific capabilities based on frequent interactions with clients, and second, that higher levels of project performance are positively correlated with higher levels of project management capabilities.

King & Tucci's (2002) considerations are also linked to the impact of existing knowledge on firms' behavior in changing markets. Investigating how capabilities arise which enable firms to succeed in changing environments King & Tucci (2002) focus their attention especially on the effect of experience in existing markets and experience of previous market entry. Similar to King & Tucci (2002), Helfat (1997) investigates the scope of firms' dynamic capability application with regard to external changes and factors such as complementary technological knowledge and physical assets.

In contrast to the previous researchers, Adner & Helfat (2003) emphasize the role of managers with reference to capability change. Adner & Helfat (2003) investigate the performance differences of companies operating in the same industries, that are, consequently, faced with the same environmental changes. Adner & Helfat (2003) postulate that the differences in firm performances appear because of capacity differences among managers working for the different companies.

Integrating the market- and resource-based view Griffith & Harvey (2001) introduce the idea of a global dynamic capability in order to extend the understanding of a firm's power in international business relationships. It is assumed that it is difficult for global dynamic capabilities to imitate combinations or resources. They provide the firm with competitive advantage by the effective coordination of inter-organizational relationships on a global base.

An examination of the data used by the above mentioned scholars illustrate the different approaches to investigate dynamic capabilities empirically : To accomplish their research efforts Henderson & Cockburn (1994) use qualitative and quantitative data from large research studies of the pharmaceutical industry. Similar to Helfat (1997) who achieves to prove the existence of dynamic capabilities based on data from the U.S. Department of Energy, Adner & Helfat (2003) use data from the Financial Reporting System of the U.S. petroleum industry. King & Tucci's (2002) analysis is based on data from the disk drive industry since the evolution of hard drives makes it possible to investigate the dynamic capability topic in terms of new market entrances. To investigate the transfer of capabilities, Zander & Kogut (1995) developed a questionnaire based on a study of 100 major Swedish innovations and distributed this questionnaire to project engineers.

In contrast to King & Tucci's (2002), Adner & Helfat's (2003), Helfat's (1997), and Zander & Kogut's (1995) empirical research contributions which are based on data over specific time periods, Marsh & Stock (2006), Griffith & Harvey (2001), and Ethiraj et al. (2005) do not use long-term studies. More concrete, based on previous research contributions, Marsh & Stock (2006) developed questionnaires which they sent to new product development professionals. To test their hypotheses Griffith & Harvey (2001) examined the relationships between the Canadian, Chilean, British, and Filipino distributors and their primary U.S. manufacturers. They collected the data through questionnaires sent to the principals of small- and medium-sized distributors. Finally, using an extensive sample of detailed project-level data from a leading firm in the global software services industry, Ethiraj et al. (2005) attempt to show the effect of capabilities on firm performance.

Corresponding to their different research focuses and the used data the research contributions also differ in their key findings: As one of the first researchers Henderson & Cockburn (1994) have been able to show empirically that 'architectural competence' is positively related to research productivity controlling besides variation in technological opportunities 'component competence'. Henderson & Cockburn's (1994) results indicate that firms which are able to integrate knowledge from wide scientific communities and to employ the key research resources through collaboration are more effective in research than firms whose research productivity is mainly based on 'component competence'. Zander & Kogut's (1995) results show, that mainly two determinants influence the time of imitation. The first indicates to what extent knowledge about manufacturing processes already exists among competitors. The second is the degree of a firm's internal continuous recombination of capabilities (the frequency of dynamic capability use) leading to an improvement of the product or the manufacturing process.

The results of King & Tucci's (2002) and Helfat's (1997) research indicate that the 'status quo' of firms influence the further development of firms. Helfat (1997) investigates the influence of rising oil prices as an external environment on the amounts of R&D spent on coal conversion. They are able to demonstrate that especially those firms that are well equipped with complementary technological knowledge and physical assets spend larger amounts of R&D on coal conversion. King & Tucci (2002), on the other hand, are able to show that firms possessing experience of previous markets are more likely to enter new ones. Additionally, the value of experience increases if firms decide to enter new markets.

Ethiraj et al. (2005) identified client-specific and project management capabilities at the project level in software services that influenced the project contributions. Furthermore, they argue that, improvements in capabilities result in improved project profitability and, that different capabilities yield to different marginal benefits. The results of Marsh & Stock's (2006) research contribution show that 'knowledge retention' and 'knowledge interpretation' activities are important capabilities to enhance a firm's capacity to apply knowledge gained by prior product development projects to current product development projects.

Adner & Helfat (2003) point out that time-varying effects associated with corporate level managerial decisions are statistically significant. Based on their analysis, Adner & Helfat (2003) are able to formulate a dynamic *managerial* capability approach explaining firms' heterogeneity due to managerial decisions. In its basics the model considers managerial human capital, managerial social capital, and managerial cognition.

On the behalf of the results of their studies, Griffith & Harvey (2001) conclude that the power of overseas distributors can be enhanced by specific relationship investments, relationship predictability, and by increasing the market knowledge gaps between overseas distributors and U.S. manufacturers.

Based on the literature review of influential empirical research contributions with regard to central elements such as research focuses, used data, and key findings, I infer that no empirical research contribution exists that investigates the nature of dynamic capabilities in an industry independent way. Consequently, a discussion should take place *if* the development of a dynamic capability construct is possible that enables the investigation of the nature of dynamic capabilities in an industry independent way. If the answer is "yes", the next step would be to discuss *how* a dynamic capability construct should be shaped to ensure an industry independent investigation of the nature of dynamic capabilities. In the following chapter, I will contribute my suggestions with regard to this challenge.

2.2.4   Dynamic Capabilities & Firm Performance

As mentioned before, the dynamic capability research field emerged to explain the value creation of firms in dynamic environments (Teece et al. 1997). Accordingly, the main aspect of this section is to examine the relation of dynamic capabilities to firm performance.

Following the basic assumptions of dynamic capability concepts in general, to achieve sustainable competitive advantage requires both, the possession of valuable resources, as the resource-based view proposes (short term perspective, e.g. Barney (1991)), and the ability to permanently and systematically minimize the gap given by the existing and value maximizing resource configuration (long-term perspective, e.g. Teece et al. (1997), Lavie (2006)). Consequently, firms endowed with the knowledge of how to deploy and redeploy resources are able to out-innovate and out-pace their competitors due to a more effective and efficient response to market change, and, therefore, are able to establish or extend competitive advantage (Ni & Wan 2008). Consequently, a major question in dynamic capability research is "to bring clarity to the notion of dynamic capabilities and their potential and realized relationships to the performance of new ventures and established companies" (Zahra et al. 2006, p.918).

Teece et al.'s (1997) clear distinction between dynamic capabilities, as the "firm's ability to integrate, build, and reconfigure internal and external competencies", and organizational routines, as "distinctive activities to be performed", points out that the influence of dynamic capabilities on firm performance functions indirectly via organizational routines (Teece et al. 1997, p.516). Zott (2003) explicitly argues that "dynamic capabilities are indirectly linked with firm performance by aiming at changing a firm's bundle of resources, operational routines, and competencies, which in turn affect economic performance" (Zott 2003, p.98).

Even though Eisenhardt & Martin's (2000) definition is similar to the aforementioned dynamic capability descriptions, there is a difference concerning the link between dynamic capabilities and firm performance in comparison to the already described notions. According to Eisenhardt & Martin's (2000), examples of dynamic capabilities are product development, strategic decision making, and alliancing. However, Eisenhardt & Martin (2000, p.1107) describe product development routines as "revenue producing products and services". Comparing these two statements, Eisenhardt & Martin's (2000) conception of dynamic capabilities seems to be ambiguous. On the one hand, dynamic capabilities are defined as "organizational and strategic routines by which firms achieve new resource configurations", on the other hand, the outcome of dynamic capabilities are products and services, *directly* generating revenues (e.g., product development).

Zahra et al.'s (2006) model is based on the idea that dynamic capabilities represent higher-order capabilities used to alter substantive capabilities (cf. section 2.2.2). The substantive capabilities, however, are defined as capacities to produce a desired output (tangible or intangible) (Winter 2003) or the "ability to solve a problem" (Zahra et al. 2006, p.921). Yet, in this context it is important to point out that Zahra et al. (2006) assume no direct link between dynamic capabilities and firm performance. The influence of dynamic capabilities on firm performance is indirect and arises in two situations: the appropriate reconfiguration of substantive capabilities and the adaptation of organizational knowledge (Zahra et al. 2006).

Helfat et al. (2007) emphasize that the effects of dynamic capabilities on firm performance must not necessarily be positive. They argue that the outcomes of the application of dynamic capabilities might fit inferiorly to the demands the resource-based view asks for in comparison to the previous resource base configuration.

2.3 Towards an Operationalization of Dynamic Capabilities

The general aim to develop a comprehensive dynamic capability framework is to explain and capture wealth creation of firms operating in changing environments (Teece et al. 1997, Teece 2007), and at the same time to provide firms' decision makers with an appropriate instrument to adapt the resource base according to the changing environment. Accordingly, conceptual research contributions are essential to develop theories, however, empirical research contributions are vital in order to verify the made assumptions.

Examining influential dynamic capability concepts (cf. section 2.2.3), I recognize that each research contribution focuses on specific characteristics or aspects of dynamic capabilities. For example, Eisenhardt & Martin (2000) highlight the dependency of dynamic capability specifications on the velocity of market change, whereas Zollo & Winter (2002) investigate the shaping process of dynamic capabilities depending on firm inherent operations such as experience accumulation, knowledge articulation, and knowledge codification processes. In this context, Zahra et al. (2006) emphasize the interrelation and co-evolution of dynamic and substantive capabilities as well as the effects of organizational age on dynamic capabilities.

Delimiting dynamic capabilities from 'ad hoc problem solving', Winter (2003), as well as Helfat & Peteraf (2003) refines the dynamic capability concept. They describe the 'aging process' of capabilities which takes place without the influence of dynamic capabilities. Similar to Makadok (2001), who investigates the effects of different modes to execute resource base changes, Lavie (2006) outlines a complex model explaining which modes of resource base reconfiguration are the best in dependence on the attributes of the considered capabilities and the nature of technological change. A more process orientated view of dynamic capabilities is represented by Zott (2003) and Teece (2007).

Briefly, all these research contributions focus on different, specific aspects of dynamic capabilities, and, therefore, contribute to a better understanding of the nature and consequences of dynamic capabilities. However, up to now a comprehensive framework that enables an industry-crossing empirical investigation of dynamic capabilities is still missing.

Reviewing the selection of empirical research contributions (cf. section 2.2.3), I notice that their theoretical foundations as well as their constructs and construct interrelations differ utterly from pure dynamic capability concepts. For instance, some research contributions reflect only parts of the dynamic capability framework (Cohen & Levinthal 1990, Zander & Kogut 1995, Marsh & Stock 2006). Others are industry specific (Henderson & Cockburn 1994), prove the existence dynamic capabilities rather than examine their nature or the interrelationship between their specific elements (Helfat 1997, Adner & Helfat 2003), or describe specific firm domains respectively phases (Griffith & Harvey 2001, King & Tucci 2002, Ethiraj et al. 2005).

These insights do not provide any reason to doubt their research significance or impact on the mentioned empirical research contributions. Yet, they demonstrate the absence of a generalizing approach to measure dynamic capabilities across industries. Similar to the development of a more general definition of dynamic capabilities, based on the conceptual dynamic capability approaches, and the experience developed from empirical research contributions, a discussion should take place how dynamic capabilities could be operationalized in an industry-crossing way.

In the following, I develop a line of reasoning to demonstrate that an empirical, industry independent investigation of the nature of dynamic capabilities is possible, and I also outline a first step towards an operationalization of dynamic capabilities.

The literature review of section 2.2.3 shows, that an appropriate adaptation of the resource base is a complex procedure incorporating different firm functionalities (Zott 2003, Lavie 2006, Teece 2007). The characteristics of dynamic capabilities may differ depending on, for instance, the velocity of market change (Eisenhardt & Martin 2000), the nature of technology change or specific attributes of the capabilities (Lavie 2006), or the capacities of managers (Adner & Helfat 2003).

However, one prerequisite for achieving competitive advantage is not only to do the 'right' thing, but to execute the 'right' thing in an efficient way. With regard to capabilities and dynamic capabilities, Zahra et al. (2006) argue that efficiency is based upon stable patterns, which strengthen with utilization. Therefore, despite the complexity of dynamic capabilities, due to the postulation of efficiency, specific dynamic capability features will arise in firms when changing the resource base in a purposeful way (Helfat et al. 2007).

Furthermore, based on Zander & Kogut's (1995) research contribution about the transfer and imitation of organizational capabilities, I conclude, that dynamic capabilities are likely to follow similar or even the same functional principles across industry boarders. Eisenhardt & Martin (2000, p. 1108) argue alike and state that "dynamic capabilities have greater equifinality, homogeneity, and substitutability across firms than traditional RBV thinking implies." Eisenhardt & Martin (2000) refer to 'best practice' to describe the industry independent functional principles of dynamic capabilities.

With regard to different dynamic capability characteristics, the challenge to operationalize dynamic capabilities means to develop a dynamic capability construct that is sufficiently abstract to capture the different characteristics of dynamic capabilities, however, which at the same time is sufficiently precise to reflect the nature of dynamic capabilities. In consideration of the complexity of dynamic capabilities (Teece et al. 1997) and their specific characteristics the best way to capture the nature of dynamic capabilities in an industry independent way seems to be the development of a most simple instrument (Eisenhardt & Martin 2000).

One possibility to approach this challenge is, first, to clarify the dimensionality of the dynamic capability construct, and, second, if existing, to specify the characteristics and elements of each sub-construct. With regard to dynamic capabilities, the demands of an institution delivering a firm's capacity to react quickly to shifting market situations can hardly be described by one omnipotent element. The mere assumption that dynamic capabilities incorporate entrepreneurial activities (Zahra et al. 2006) leads imperatively to the conclusion that dynamic capabilities must be considered as an institution comprising different facets. In other words, a dynamic capability concept can hardly be reflected or even operationalized by an uni-dimensional construct. A comprehensive operationalization of dynamic capabilities can only be accomplished by the development of a multi-dimensional construct.

Following different authors (Teece 2007, Zott 2003) a first partition of dynamic capabilities should consider the processes of identification and response formulation. Helfat et al. (2007, p.2) support this argumentation highlighting that dynamic capabilities enable firms "to identify the need or opportunity for change, formulate a response to such a need or opportunity, and implement a course of action". Following their statement the functionality of dynamic capabilities can be split up into three major abilities. The first ability is the process of identification in which a firm permanently examines its environment in order to recognize threats and opportunities. Applying the second ability - the process of response formulation that the firm develops - assesses alternatives and lastly, determines the way to react in a given situation. The third ability, the process of implementation is characterized by the execution of the chosen tasks.

Other researchers follow a similar approach to describe the functionality of dynamic capabilities. For instance, Zott (2003) subdivides the resource configuration process into 'variation', 'selection', and 'retention', Teece (2007) distinguishes between (1) sensing and shaping opportunities and threats, (2) seizing opportunities, and (3) enhancing, combining, protecting, and reconfiguring assets (cf. section 2.2.3). In consideration of Teece's (2007) detailed and practical description of each of these elements without losing reference to theoretical considerations, a first subdivision of the dynamic capability construct should be given by 'sensing', 'seizing', and 'reconfiguring'.

In contrast to Katkalo et al. (2010) who state that dynamic capabilities can be classified "wether they support sensing, seizing, or transforming" (Katkalo et al. 2010, p.1179), I argue that dynamic capabilities consist of these three sub-dimensions. Rather, the application of these sub-dimensions of dynamic capabilities in order to purposefully change a firms resource base (Helfat et al. 2007) takes place in a specific time order starting with 'sensing' and ending with 'reconfiguring'. This approach to understand dynamic capabilities as a process reflects Zott's (2003) as well as Helfat et al.'s (2007) interpretation of dynamic capabilities and highlights the importance of each sub-dimension with reference to the results of applied dynamic capabilities.

When, how, and with what intensity firms use these sub-dimensions is a function of the path (Teece et al. 1997), the status quo of the resource base (Zahra et al. 2006), of the managerial capacities of a firm's decision makers (Adner & Helfat 2003, Teece 2007), and external factors such as the velocity of market change (Eisenhardt & Martin 2000).

2.4 Discussion, Limitations & Future Research of the First Research Objective

Analyzing conceptual and empirical research contributions it becomes obvious that though efforts have been made to clarify the notion of dynamic capabilities and their terminology (Helfat et al. 2007), there still remain significant uncertainties with regard to their meaning and functioning (Schreyögg & Kliesch-Eberl 2007).

Equally, a central research gap still exist: A comprehensive and generally accepted conceptualization of dynamic capabilities that serves as an instrument to investigate these firm inherent institutions empirically in an industry crossing way has not yet been developed (cf. 2.2.3). Indeed, there are research efforts to investigate dynamic capabilities empirically, however most, of these investigations are data-driven and, therefore, industry specific (cf. section 2.2.3).

Since the dynamic capability approach is most promising to reveal the long-term competitive advantage of firms, it is of academic interest to close this research gap (Teece et al. 1997). Even so, the practical consequences are evident. Given a conceptual model whose validity across firms and industries has been proven empirically, researchers are able to derive principles of how firms should behave in fast changing environments to maintain or even increase competitive advantage (Teece 2007).

Based on the empirical results of Zander & Kogut (1995), in section 2.3, I argue in accordance with Eisenhardt & Martin (2000) that because of the postulation of effectiveness, an industry-crossing operationalization of dynamic capabilities must be possible.

Furthermore, I argue that a dynamic capability construct must consist of different sub-constructs. Since Teece (2007) outlines a process orientated dynamic capability framework built upon 'sensing', 'seizing', and 'reconfiguration', and at the same time refers to practical issues, I consider his contribution as a promising way towards developing a commonly accepted dynamic capability construct. Based on these sub-constructs I propose a process-orientated approach to describe dynamic capabilities across industries.

In recent literature, efforts have been made to develop conceptions that are appropriate to measure dynamic capabilities across industries. For instance, Wang & Ahmed (2007) propose a dynamic capability construct consisting of 'adaptive capability', 'absorptive capability', and 'innovative capability' that support firm specific processes such as integration, reconfiguration, renewal, and recreation. To ensure the strategic implications of dynamic capabilities - in contrast to my proposition of a process orientated dynamic capability approach - Wang & Ahmed (2007) stress their assumption, that dynamic capabilities are not processes, but embedded in processes[4]. However, the line of reasoning should be the other way around: The first step should be to understand the nature of dynamic capabilities, and only then the strategic implications of the results should be discussed.

A further critical issue is the closeness of constructs such as the adaptive capability as the "firm's the ability to identify and capitalize on emerging market opportunities" (Wang & Ahmed 2007, p.37) to the absorptive capability as "the firm's ability to recognize the

---

[4]Wang & Ahmed (2007) assume, that processes are often explicitly known and, therefore, can be transferred easier across firm boundaries. A counterexample of Wang & Ahmed's (2007) assumptions is the well described new product development process of a car.

value of new, external information, assimilate it, and apply it to commercial ends" (Cohen & Levinthal 1990, p.128).

Ambrosini & Bowman (2009) summarize a number of factors that shape dynamic capabilities and consequently influence the effective employment of dynamic capabilities such as existing resources (Zollo & Winter 2002), social capital (Blyler & Coff 2003), leadership (Rosenbloom 2000), the role of managers (Adner & Helfat 2003, Harreld et al. 2007), as well as external factors (Eisenhardt & Martin 2000). However, Ambrosini & Bowman (2009) fail to explain how these factors cooperate to make dynamic capabilities function and how they can be measured.

Barreto (2010) defines a dynamic capability as "the firm's potential to systematically solve problems by its [1] propensity to sense opportunities and threats, [2] to make timely and [3] market-oriented decisions, and [4] to change its resource base" (Barreto 2010, p.271). Equally to my proposition Barreto (2010) considers dynamic capabilities as a multi-dimensional construct. With reference to past researches (Pablo et al. 2007, Gilbert 2006, Menguc & Auh 2006) he also assumes that the functionality of dynamic capabilities depends largely on the existence and application of all sub-dimensions. However, Barreto (2010) assumes that the aim of dynamic capabilities is to solve problems in a systematical way[5], whereas the change of the firm's resource base is an essential capacity to do so. This stands in contrast to the general understanding of dynamic capabilities (cf. section

---

[5]Barreto (2010) uses this formulation to emphasize the difference to 'ad hoc problem solving' and 'luck' listed as alternatives to dynamic capabilities (Winter 2003). Because of the analogy, at first view, this assumption seems to be correct. However, since this formulation suggests that dynamic capabilities are of a rather reactive nature it captures only a part of dynamic capabilities. In contrast, assuming that dynamic capabilities are capable to increase competitive advantage, dynamic capabilities must largely be driven by pro-active elements.

2.2.2). In previous research contributions authors hold the opinion, that the aim of dynamic capabilities is to change the resource base (e.g. Helfat et al. (2007)). Accordingly, the central research question rather is how to change the resource base in a way that maintains or even enlarges competitive advantage. Additionally, the remaining dimensions Barreto (2010) specifies are externally orientated and ignore the possibility of resource base changes independent of external conditions.

With regard to the above mentioned issues, I propose a multi-dimensional construct (Barreto 2010) consisting of the dimensions 'sensing', 'seizing', and 'reconfiguring' (Teece 2007) that reflects the notion of process orientation is most promising. A first literature review with regard to the three-dimensional dynamic capability construct developed above to provide appropriate insights or even instruments to investigate each of these sub-constructs deliver some results (Cohen & Levinthal 1990, Amit & Schoemaker 1993, Weick & Roberts 1993, Iansiti & Clark 1994, Malone & Crowston 1994, Slater & Narver 1995, Hurley & Hult 1998, Van den Bosch, Volberda & de Boer 1999, Helfat & Raubitschek 2000). However, in contrast to Wang & Ahmed's (2007) and Barreto's (2010) conceptualization, which refers to exiting constructs, the first results of my literature review do not reflect the proposed dynamic capability sub-dimensions in a comprehensive way.

In other words, a limitation of my model is that a development of each sub-construct from scratch, supported by insights of dynamic capability research (cf. section 2.2.3 and 2.3) - especially by Teece's (2007) research contribution - seems to be inevitable to obtain a comprising but also 'lean' description of dynamic capabilities.

As detailed ideas of the nature of dynamic capabilities exist, a first empirical approach to investigate the nature of dynamic capabilities does not necessarily have to be limited to pure explorative techniques. Moreover, the application of methods to examine the nature of dynamic capabilities should comprise qualitative, as well as quantitative aspects.

An approach which meets both requirements is the repertory grid technique. Even though this method has, to the best of my knowledge, not yet been applied to investigate specific issues with regard to dynamic capability research, it seems to be a suitable instrument to detect specific elements that a dynamic capability construct may comprise.

George A. Kelly, who was a clinical psychologist and mathematician, developed the repertory grid technique in 1955 (Kelly 1955). The development of this technique is based on a personal construct theory: individuals perceive reality differently, which is reflected in 'mental models'. Due to the insight that the nature of dynamic capabilities depends on managerial capital (Adner & Helfat 2003), this method seems to be very suitable to investigate which elements firms' decision makers deem to be essential to be adapted to the resource base of a firm appropriate in a changing environment.

To summarize, in chapter 2 I introduced the subject of dynamic capability research to the reader. Furthermore, I analyzed a selected number of empirical contributions with reference to the dynamic capability research. Regarding the conceptual and empirical research contributions there does not exist a comprehensive understanding of the nature of dynamic capabilities. However, due to the postulation of effectiveness, I argue, that an across industry boarder investigation of dynamic capabilities must be possible. Based on conceptual research contributions I outline a first step to operationalize dynamic capabilities.

The literature review of chapter 2 also shows that no research contributions exist referring to the value that dynamic capabilities present. Therefore, in the following chapter I apply a formal approach to investigate specific research questions with regard to the value of dynamic capabilities. More concrete, in chapter 3, I investigate the value of dynamic capabilities, the influence factors as well as the consequences on firm value with regard to their application in terms of time. Even though this research question is of a rather epistemological nature, the derived insights may lead to a different view of firm value estimation.

Chapter 3

Second Research Objective: Value Implications of Dynamic Capabilities*

Dynamic capabilities are essential for a purposeful change of a firm's resource base and, therefore, are key value drivers for companies operating in changing environments. In this chapter, I investigate the value drivers of dynamic capabilities and the influence of dynamic capabilities on the value of firms. For these purposes, it is sufficient to assume that the firm's resource base is designed to support two capabilities. Since the future value generation of both capabilities is largely driven by external factors, and, therefore, cannot be exactly predicted, I model the value generation of both capabilities by means of exogenously given stochastic processes. To maximize its value, the firm possesses the ability to change its resource base by discarding (exit option) and by extending (growth option) the existing capabilities. The results show that the value of a firm is not only given by the expected value, generated by the firm's resource base in place, but also by the firm's options to react to environmental changes. Since, by definition, dynamic capabilities enable a firm to purposefully detect and execute these options, I am able to analyze different value determining factors of dynamic capabilities. In particular, the application of dynamic capabilities in terms of time has consequences on the expected value generation. These results reveal the potential impact of dynamic capabilities on the value estimation of firms as well as the importance of an appropriate application of dynamic capabilities in terms of time.

---

*I would like to thank Prof. Dr. Baldauf and Prof. Dr. Dockner for their valuable suggestions and constructive proposals which they made during the phases of model construction and implementation.

3.1 Introduction to the Second Research Objective

By reconfiguring the current resource base according to new requirements caused by environmental changes, dynamic capabilities are essential to ensure a firms' long-living (Teece et al. 1997, Eisenhardt & Martin 2000, Lavie 2006, Teece 2007).

Over the years, progresses in dynamic capabilities research have been made, for instance, when examining the nature of dynamic capabilities (Eisenhardt & Martin 2000, Teece et al. 1997, Zollo & Winter 2002), the mode of action (Zahra et al. 2006, Schreyögg & Kliesch-Eberl 2007), or cost issues (Winter 2003). Despite the fact that value maximization of firms is a central topic in strategic management research, there exists only a limited knowledge concerning the value implications of dynamic capabilities. No doubt, in the last years a discussion took place if and how dynamic capabilities influence the performance respectively the competitive advantage of firms (cf. section 2.2.4).

For instance, Teece et al. (1997) make a clear distinction between dynamic capabilities as the "firm's ability to integrate, build, and reconfigure internal and external competencies" (Teece et al. 1997, p.516) and organizational routines that are responsible to generate the firms' performance. Similar, Zahra et al. (2006) assume that dynamic capabilities are developed to alter substantive capabilities whereas substantive capabilities are developed to perform the wanted output. Despite the 'equifinality' of dynamic capabilities Eisenhardt & Martin (2000) assume that dynamic capabilities have an indirect effect on competitive advantage.

Until now, however, in the dynamic capability field there still is a discussion missing *if* dynamic capabilities influence firm value, even in a "dormant" state, and if "yes", *what* value dynamic capabilities possess. Furthermore, what are the value driving factors of dynamic capabilities? What influence does the point in time at which a resource base modification is executed have on the value of dynamic capabilities and firm value?

To provide answers to these research questions, I have developed a mathematical model incorporating knowledge from the dynamic capability and the real options research field. Real options research provides appropriate instruments to identify the value maximizing points in time, when to execute a resource base change, as well as their determinants. Consequently, applying knowledge from both research fields, I am able to show the close interrelatedness between the value of dynamic capabilities and the value of options calculated by real options models.

More concrete, based on the works of Kogut & Kulatilaka (2001) and Kyläheiko et al. (2002), I assume that the value of a dynamic capability is equal to the option value to discard or modify capabilities: In my model, I focus on a firm's resource base used to support the value generation of two capabilities. In order to maximize the firm's value generation the firm can follow the policy to discard or extend its capabilities. I argue that the firm's ability to detect the value maximizing point in time and to execute the capability change is the inherent task, or in other words the intrinsic reason for the existence of dynamic capabilities (Helfat et al. 2007).

The results of the analytical examination of my model show, that the value of a dynamic capability is given by the option value to modify the resource base. Consequently, I can identify and measure the value determining factors of dynamic capabilities. Assuming that firms are value maximizers, the findings furthermore show that there is an optimal timing to execute a capability change. This enables me to calculate the value consequences of a suboptimal application of dynamic capabilities in terms of time.

Additionally, even though I can show that dynamic capabilities themselves do not generate value, the possession of dynamic capabilities influences the value of a firm. This insight, derived from the results of my model supports the importance of dynamic capability research and may have an impact on the existing approaches to estimate the value of firms.

These results deepen and extend the existing knowledge of dynamic capabilities and even proof made assumptions as wrong (Eisenhardt & Martin 2000). Even though the main focus of this research objective is of a rather epistemological nature, there are also normative implication. For instance, since I demonstrate that dynamic capabilities - even if not applied - influence the value of firms managers should reconsider the development of dynamic capabilities with regard to cost issues (Winter 2003). The model also shows, that the value of a firm depends on the point in time dynamic capabilities are applied. This insight should make managers use dynamic capabilities in well thought out ways with regard to timing (Eisenhardt & Martin 2000).

The remainder of this chapter is organized as follows. In section 3.2, I briefly introduce the basic ideas of the real option research to the reader, in section 3.3, I outline the mathematical model. Based on its results formulated as a theorem, in section 3.4, I infer different propositions concerning the value of dynamic capabilities. In the last part of this research contribution I discuss the results, deepen the academic and normative implications of my model, show limitations and outline future research avenues.

3.2   Real Options

A real option is seen as the investment in uncertain physical, or human assets with the awareness that the decision is irreversible concerning future contingent events (Kogut & Kulatilaka 1994). Central to the real option perspective is the question whether these investments are useful not only with regard to current, but also to future applications. Therefore, strategic investment decisions must consider the market, as well as the position of the firm (Kogut & Kulatilaka 2001).

To evaluate such investments, the traditional corporate finance literature suggests to apply instruments such as the discounted cash flow model. However, when applying these instruments the value of flexibility is not considered (Bowman & Moskowitz 2001). Recognizing this problem, the real options approach is used as a strategic decision-making and capital budgeting tool, as it explicitly accounts for the value of future flexibility (Amram & Kulatilaka 1999). Therefore, strategy researchers have suggested to make specific strategic decisions with reference to instruments of real options (Hurry, Miller & Bowman 1992, Hurry 1993, Kester 1984, Kogut 1991).

To enhance the quality of the decision making process concerning these investments, a well-developed set of instruments mainly applied in financial economics has been developed (Dixit 1992). In its simplest form, the real option process consists of three steps: 1. selection of and the investment in an option, 2. evaluation of the options, and 3. expansion of the option triggered by an external or internal signal (Bowman & Hurry 1993). Thereby, each investment stage (e.g. in technology development or venture capital) can be interpreted as an option of further investments (Trigeorgis 1993). Analogous to financial options the firm receives the right, but not the obligation, to execute a future capability changes (Amram & Kulatilaka 1999).

Within the strategic management context, the real options theory has been adopted to gain deeper insights into certain issues. For instance, McGrath (1997) applies the real options theory to technologically positioned projects and examines the dependence of the value of the technology option on boundary conditions and uncertainty. Kogut & Kulatilaka (2004) use the real options theory to resolve valuation and implementation problems in organizations. Regarding joint ventures, Kogut (1991) has demonstrated the strategic relevance of real options from a theoretical as well as from an empirical perspective. Further, Childs & Triantis (1999) show the use of the real options theory to analyze investments in R&D. Bowman & Hurry (1993) have developed a heuristic method that can be used in strategic management in which they integrate resource allocation, organizational learning, and strategic positioning. The real options theory has also been applied in venture capital investments and capital budgeting (Dixit & Pindyck 1994, Hurry et al. 1992).

In this chapter, I apply knowledge from real option research to investigate the implications of the existence and the timely application of dynamic capabilities on firms' value. More concrete, I demonstrate that the value of flexibility calculated by the application of a real options approach is equal to the value of the deployed dynamic capability.

3.3   Model Description & Mathematical Specification

The mathematical model is designed to use an imaginary firm that operates with a given resource base consisting of two distinct capabilities, denoted by x and y. The firm uses both capabilities to generate value. The values of each capability are derived from two exogenous price processes denoted by θ_x and θ_y, that follow a Geometric Brownian Motion (GBM),

$$d\theta_x(t) = \mu_x\theta_x(t)dt + \sigma_x\theta_x(t)dW_x(t), \qquad (3.1)$$

$$d\theta_y(t) = \mu_y\theta_y(t)dt + \sigma_y\theta_y(t)dW_y(t). \qquad (3.2)$$

The parameters μ_i denote the time-invariant drift rates, σ_i the time-invariant volatilities, and $dW_i(t)$ the Wiener increments of the stochastic processes $\theta_i(t)$, $i = x, y$. $\theta_x(t)$ and $\theta_y(t)$ are the price processes related to the capabilities x and y. I define the starting values of $\theta_x(t = 0)$ and $\theta_y(t = 0)$ by θ_{x0}, respectively θ_{y0}. Employing capability x with intensity α $(0 < \alpha < 1)$, the value generated in period t is given by $\alpha\theta_x(t)$. It is assumed that the two exogenous processes have distinct long-run properties. Since future values generated by the capabilities x and y are less worthwhile for the firm, I use the risk less interest rate r $(r > 0)$ to discount the in the future generated values. While capability x

is a diminishing capability and, therefore, is reflected by a negative expected value change $(\mu_x < 0)$, capability y possesses a positive expected value change reflected by $\mu_y > 0$. To ensure the solvability of the model, I am furthermore forced to assume $\mu_y < r$.

When using the existing resource base in order to apply the capabilities x and y a firm can face one of three possible environments. It can implement the resource base as it is and face stochastically changing firm values due to changes in the values of $\theta_x(t)$ and $\theta_y(t)$, but with no adjustments of the resource base and the corresponding capabilities. This reference firm serves as a benchmark. The existing resource base is the only value driver of the reference firm.

Alternatively, a firm can face a dynamic environment in which it is able to adjust flexibly to both, the diminishing and the growing capability. In this case, the firm employs dynamic capabilities and optimally adjusts its resource base. Dynamic capabilities arise from the option to adjust the resource base (either by scaling down or by upgrading an existing capability). Exercising these options optimally has value implications that are in the focus of this paper.

Finally, a firm can face a dynamic environment in which it adjusts its resource base, but in a suboptimal manner.

In the reference case, I assume that the firm employs capability x with intensity α and capability y with intensity $(1-\alpha)c_0$. The value of the firm in this scenario is given by

$$V_{RB}(\theta_x, \theta_y) \equiv E\left\{ \int_0^\infty [\alpha\,\theta_x + c_0(1-\alpha)\theta_y]\,e^{-rt} dt \right\}. \tag{3.3}$$

The firm value $V_{RB}(\theta_x, \theta_y)$ measures the value of the resource base. It consists of the sum of the expected present values of capabilities x and y.

Reacting to external changes and adjusting its given capabilities by exercising contraction or expansion options, the firm applies its *dynamic capabilities*. In case of dynamic capabilities, I assume that the firm abandons capability x and concentrates on resources around capability y, so that the intensity of y changes from $(1-\alpha)c_0$ to c_0. In addition, I assume that the firm has the option to expand capability y from $c_0\theta_y(t)$ to $qc_0\theta_y(t)$ with $q > 1$. Hence, in this model dynamic capabilities are assigned to (i) a complete pull out from capability x and a reallocation to y, and (ii) an expansion of y. Releasing resources from capability x generates a constant salvage value (SV), while expanding capability y from $(1-\alpha)c_0$ to $q(1-\alpha)c_0$ results in investment costs given by $q(1-\alpha)IC$.

Using a firm's dynamic capabilities optimally, which in this context means to exercise its contraction and expansion options optimally, the firm maximizes its value given by

$$
\begin{aligned}
V_{Max}(\theta_x, \theta_y) \;=\; & \max E\Bigg\{\int_0^{\tau_1} \left[\alpha\theta_x(t) + c_0(1-\alpha)\theta_y(t)\right]e^{-rt}dt + SVe^{-\tau_1} \\
& + \int_{\tau_1}^{\tau_2} c_0\theta_y(t)e^{-r(t-\tau_2)}dt - qICe^{-\tau_2} + \int_{\tau_2}^{\infty} qc_0\theta_y e^{-r(t-\tau_2)}dt\Bigg\}.
\end{aligned} \tag{3.4}
$$

The firm derives value over an initial period, $[0, \tau_1)$, through the optimal use of its given resource base, generates additional value over the period $[\tau_1, \tau_2)$ through the focus on the growing capability y, and generates value over the period $[\tau_2, \infty)$ through the expansion of capability y. This interpretation assumes that the contraction and expansion options are sequentially exercised.

The exercise dates τ_1 and τ_2 are chosen optimally as to maximize the firm value (3.4). Sometimes it might be the case that firms exercise their dynamic capabilities, but choose suboptimal exercise dates. In this case the value function (3.4) has to be changed to account for the suboptimal $\tilde{\tau}_1$ and $\tilde{\tau}_2$. Following a standard real options approach, the optimal exercise date τ_1 is defined as the first passage when the process $\theta_x(t)$ hits the threshold level $\bar{\theta}_x$. Alternatively, the date τ_2 is defined as the first passage when the process $\theta_y(t)$ hits the threshold $\bar{\theta}_y$. The choice of the two threshold levels is endogenous and driven by the properties of the price processes $\theta_x(t)$ and $\theta_y(t)$, the salvage value SV, and the investment costs IC. In general, I distinguish two alternative cases, one in which the dissolution of capability x occurs first and is followed by an expansion of y from $c_0\theta_y(t)$ to $qc_0\theta_y(t)$, and the other, in which the expansion of y occurs first followed by abandoning capability x. In this case the expansion of y is from $(1-\alpha)c_0$ to $q(1-\alpha)c_0$ and triggers investment costs at a level of $(1-\alpha)IC$.

3.4 Dynamic Capabilities, Firm Value & Driving Factors

3.4.1 Value Maximizing Timing

Depending on the values of θ_i and $\bar{\theta}_i$, four different value states of the firm may arise: the first one, characterized by a cash flow generation of $\theta_x > \bar{\theta}_x$ and $\theta_y < \bar{\theta}_y$, is given by the firm's application of capability x with the intensity of α and capability y with the intensity of $(1-\alpha)c_0$, however, it possesses the options to discard capability x and to extend capability y. I now assume that the value of θ_y reaches the trigger value $\bar{\theta}_y$, inducing the firm to execute its option to extend capability y. Hence, the firm's value is given by the value generation of capability x applied with the intensity of α, the value generation of capability y with the intensity of $(1-\alpha)qc_0$, and the option value to discard capability x.

However, before θ_y reaches $\bar{\bar{\theta}}_y$, θ_x might reach $\bar{\theta}_x$. This directs the firm to execute its option to discard capability x to the benefits of capability y. In this constellation, the firm's value is given by the application of capability y with the intensity c_0 plus the option value to extend this capability. Starting from this situation, a value of θ_y reaching $\bar{\bar{\theta}}_y$ causes the firm to execute its option to extend capability y. Accordingly, the new firm value is only given by the value generation of capability y with the intensity qc_0. Figure 3.1 shows the two possible paths to reach the final value state.

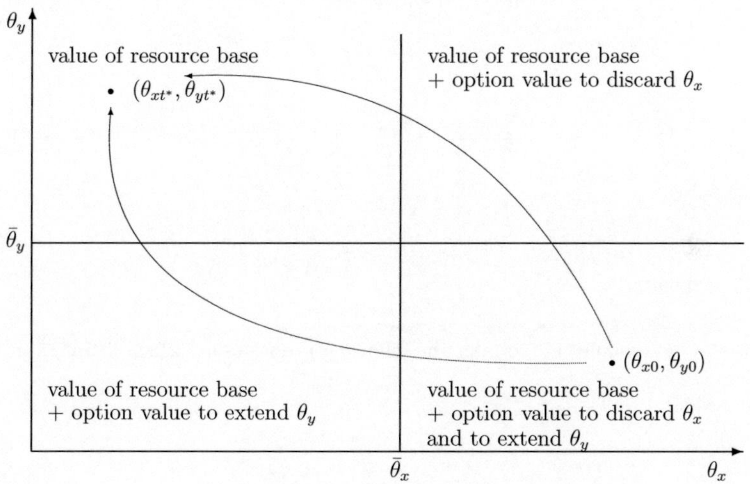

Figure 3.1: Path of capability change

I summarize these deliberations in the following theorem:

THEOREM *With reference to my model and under the assumption that the firm is able to optimally employ its dynamic capabilities, the firm value is a function of θ_x and θ_y and given by*

$$V_{Max}(\theta_x, \theta_y) = \begin{cases} \underbrace{\dfrac{\alpha}{r-\mu_x}\theta_x + \dfrac{(1-\alpha)c_0}{r-\mu_y}\theta_y}_{\text{value of resource base}} + \underbrace{A\theta_x^\gamma + B\theta_y^\varepsilon}_{\text{value of flexiblity}} & : \quad \theta_x > \bar{\theta}_x \wedge \theta_y < \bar{\theta}_y \\[2em] \underbrace{\dfrac{\alpha}{r-\mu_x}\theta_x + \dfrac{(1-\alpha)qc_0}{r-\mu_y}\theta_y}_{\text{value of resource base}} + \underbrace{A\theta_x^\gamma}_{\text{value of flexbility}} & : \quad \theta_x > \bar{\theta}_x \wedge \theta_y > \bar{\theta}_y \\[2em] \underbrace{\dfrac{c_0}{r-\mu_y}\theta_y}_{\text{value of resource base}} + \underbrace{B\theta_y^\varepsilon}_{\text{value of flexiblity}} & : \quad \theta_x < \bar{\theta}_x \wedge \theta_y < \bar{\theta}_y \\[2em] \underbrace{\dfrac{qc_0}{r-\mu_y}\theta_y}_{\text{value of resource base}} & : \quad \theta_x < \bar{\theta}_x \wedge \theta_y > \bar{\theta}_y, \end{cases}$$

(3.5)

with

$$A = \frac{\alpha}{\gamma(\mu_x-r)}\bar{\theta}_x^{(1-\gamma)} \quad ; \quad \gamma = \frac{1}{2} - \frac{\mu_x}{\sigma_x^2} - \sqrt{\left(\frac{1}{2} - \frac{\mu_x}{\sigma_x^2}\right)^2 + \frac{2r}{\sigma_x^2}} \quad ; \quad \bar{\theta}_x = \frac{r-\mu_x}{\alpha}\frac{\gamma}{\gamma-1}SV$$

$$B = \frac{c_0(q-1)}{\varepsilon(r-\mu_y)}\bar{\theta}_y^{(1-\varepsilon)} \quad ; \quad \varepsilon = \frac{1}{2} - \frac{\mu_y}{\sigma_y^2} + \sqrt{\left(\frac{1}{2} - \frac{\mu_y}{\sigma_y^2}\right)^2 + \frac{2r}{\sigma_y^2}} \quad ; \quad \bar{\theta}_y = \frac{\varepsilon}{\varepsilon-1}\frac{r-\mu_y}{c_0(q-1)}qIC.$$

(3.6)

PROOF Cf. appendix A.

This theorem enables me to infer the following propositions, which I discuss in the following sections.

3.4.2 Components of Firm Value

The first proposition, which I can formulate based on the theorem, reads as follows:

PROPOSITION 1 *The value of a firm is determined by the sum of the values generated by its resource base and the firm's flexibility to change the resource base.*

Examining the first solution of equation 3.5, I notice that the firm's maximal value $V_{Max}(\theta_x, \theta_y)$ is achieved by the optimal application of the firm's dynamic capabilities, that consist of four different value components. The first term $\frac{\alpha}{r-\mu_x}\theta_x$ represents the expected, accumulated, discounted value of capability x in use. Analogous to the expected value generation of capability x, the value generation of capability y is described by $\frac{(1-\alpha)c_0}{r-\mu_y}\theta_y$. In this case capability y is applied with the scope $(1 - \alpha)c_0$, etc.

The value of flexibility to discard capability x is given by $A\theta_x^\gamma$, and the value of flexibility to extend capability y is given by $B\theta_y^\varepsilon$. In sum, the expected value of a firm consists of the expected value generated by its existing capabilities and the flexibility value to change its capabilities.

3.4.3 Value of Firms' Dynamic Capabilities & Flexibility

Since the value of flexibility is equal to the option values to execute changes and since dynamic capabilities are essential to execute resource base changes purposefully (Helfat et al. 2007), and, therefore, represent the firm's ability to react flexible on environmental shifts by the use of organizational and strategic routines, the option value to execute changes is equal to the value of dynamic capabilities applied to fulfill the intended changes. I summarize this result in proposition 2.

> PROPOSITION 2 *The option value to modify a capability is equal to the value of the dynamic capability applied to accomplish the capability change.*

In essence, the extension of capability y corresponds to an American call option, the abandonment of capability x to an American put option.

The results also show, that contrary to capabilities, dynamic capabilities themselves do not generate *material* value. Dynamic capabilities are rather essential to hone "internal technological, organizational, and managerial processes inside the firm" (Teece et al. 1997, p. 509). However, through my model I am able to assign a specific value to the firm's capacity to modify its resource base. For instance, capability y provides the expected material value $\frac{c_0}{r-\mu_y}\theta_y$. The value of the option and, therefore, the monetary evaluation of the dynamic capability applied to extend capability y from scope c_0 to scope qc_0, is given by $B\theta_y^\varepsilon$. After the extension the expected value generation of capability y is $\frac{qc_0}{r-\mu_y}\theta_y$.

This result - based on a mathematical model - that dynamic capabilities themselves, contrary to capabilities, do not generate value, but enable the firm to optimize the resource base supports the assumptions of different scholars such as Teece et al. (1997), Eisenhardt & Martin (2000), Helfat & Peteraf (2003), or Winter (2003). Additionally, I have to emphasize that the values of the new capability constellations are expected values. These results are also in accordance with the dynamic capability literature, since the application of dynamic capabilities does not necessarily lead to performance improvements (Helfat et al. 2007).

3.4.4 Driving Factors of Dynamic Capability Value

Driving forward the insights of section 3.4.3, I am able to define the value of a dynamic capability to extend an existing capability by V_{DC_y}, and which - in the context of my model assumptions - is given by $V_{DC_y} = B\theta_y^\varepsilon$. Accordingly, I am able to define the value of a dynamic capability enabling a firm to discard a capability by V_{DC_x}, and which - also in the context of my model - is given by $V_{DC_x} = A\theta_x^\gamma$. Following these considerations I can identify the value drivers of dynamic capability:

> PROPOSITION 3 *Based on the insights of the sections 3.4.1 and 3.4.3, the value of a dynamic capability depends on the a) expected drift rate μ, b) the market volatility σ, c) the extend of the investment q correlated with the investment costs qIC, or the salvage value SV, and d) the current value θ (underlying assets).*

Interested in the effectiveness of the identified influence factors on dynamic capability value, I exemplarily carry out some simulations.

3.4.4.1 Value Consequences of Driving Factors on V_{DC_x}

The value of a dynamic capability V_{DC_x} enabling a firm to discard a capability is a function of the expected market development μ_x, the volatility of the market σ_x, the scope of the capability α, as well as the salvage value SV the firms obtain discarding the capability.

Composing the different parameters, I obtain equation 3.7 for V_{DC_x}:

$$V_{DC_x} = A\theta_x^{\gamma} = \frac{SV}{-\frac{1}{2}+\frac{\mu_x}{\sigma_x^2}+\sqrt{\left(\frac{1}{2}-\frac{\mu_x}{\sigma_x^2}\right)^2+\frac{2r}{\sigma_x^2}}}$$

$$\left(SV\frac{r-\mu_x}{\alpha}\frac{\frac{1}{2}-\frac{\mu_x}{\sigma_x^2}-\sqrt{\left(\frac{1}{2}-\frac{\mu_x}{\sigma_x^2}\right)^2+\frac{2r}{\sigma_x^2}}}{\frac{1}{2}-\frac{\mu_x}{\sigma_x^2}-\sqrt{\left(\frac{1}{2}-\frac{\mu_x}{\sigma_x^2}\right)^2+\frac{2r}{\sigma_x^2}}-1}\theta_x^{-1}\right)^{-\left(\frac{1}{2}-\frac{\mu_x}{\sigma_x^2}-\sqrt{\left(\frac{1}{2}-\frac{\mu_x}{\sigma_x^2}\right)^2+\frac{2r}{\sigma_x^2}}\right)}. \qquad (3.7)$$

To investigate the influence of μ_x, σ_x, SV on V_{DC_x}, the most efficient way is to picture V_{DC_x} as a function of θ_x (as the only time variant variable), and as one further parameter, while the remaining ones are considered as being constant.

The following calculations are based on $r = 6\%$, $\theta_{x0} = 5$, $\alpha = 0.9$, $SV = 10$, $\mu_x = -5\%$, $\sigma_x = 15\%$, leading to $\gamma = -0.8476$ and $\bar{\theta}_x = 0.56071$. The values are chosen on the basis of simulations providing realistic results of first passage times.

With respect to the following simulations, I choose the domain $\theta_x = [\bar{\theta}_x, \theta_{x0}]$ for the actual cash flow generated by capability x. However, since $\bar{\theta}_x$ is a function of μ_x, σ_x, SV, I have to stress that $\bar{\theta}_x$ represents only in connection with the standard values of μ_x, σ_x, and SV the value maximizing trigger bound. Nevertheless, based on the simulations, I am able to recognize fundamental effects of different parameters on the value of dynamic capabilities.

The first step is to analyze the development of the dynamic capability value V_{DC_x} in dependence of the domain $\mu_x = [-10\%, -1\%]$ and θ_x. Figure 3.2 shows the results.

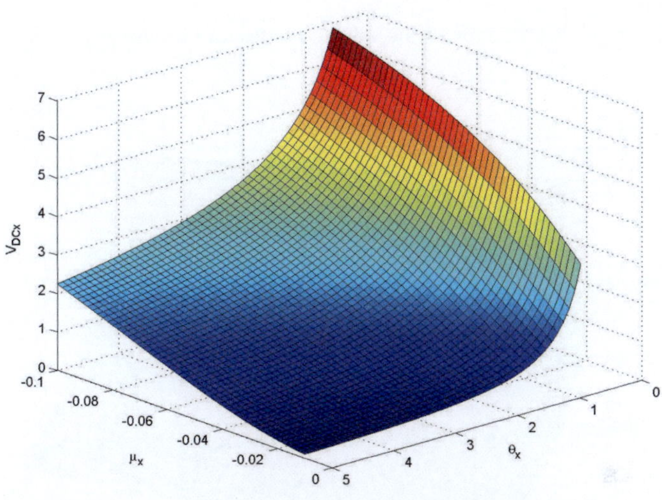

Figure 3.2: The value of the dynamic capability V_{DC_x} as a function of θ_x and μ_x

The combination of a small decreasing rate of the expected value generation of capability x, and high values of the actual value generation of capability x leads to small dynamic capability values V_{DC_x}. Higher expected decreasing rates of μ_x of the value generation θ_x in combination with high actual value generation of capability x, leads to an approximately linear increase of the dynamic capability value V_{DC_x}. In the case of small decreasing rates $\mu_x > -0.02$ and high capability value generation ($\theta_x > 2$), the value of the dynamic capability to discard capability x remains close to 0. Indeed, a value variation of θ_x in the range of $\theta_x = [2,5]$ has an inferior impact on V_{DC_x}. However, a further decrease of θ_x leads to an exponential increase of V_{DC_x}.

Figure 3.3 shows the dynamic capability value V_{DC_x} as a function of θ_x and the assumed volatility $\sigma_x = [1\%, 25\%]$ of the value generation of θ_x. As expected, the dynamic

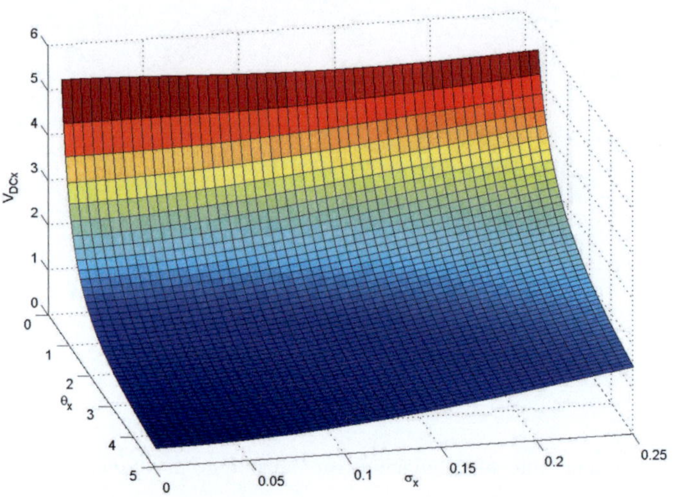

Figure 3.3: The value of the dynamic capability V_{DC_x} as a function of θ_x and σ_x

capability value V_{DC_x} increases with θ_x approaching the trigger bound $\bar{\theta}_x$ to discard capability x, supported by an increase of σ_x. However, θ_x approaching the trigger bound $\bar{\theta}_x$, the effect of σ_x wanes.

Figure 3.4 deals with the variation of the salvage value SV ($SV = [1, 20]$) in combination with θ_x. The results show, that the value of the dynamic capability depends largely on the salvage value SV, which the firm obtains by discarding capability x. In the case of small salvage values (in my case $SV < 5$), the value of the dynamic capability x is close to 0, independent of the value generation θ_x of capability x. Increasing salvage values

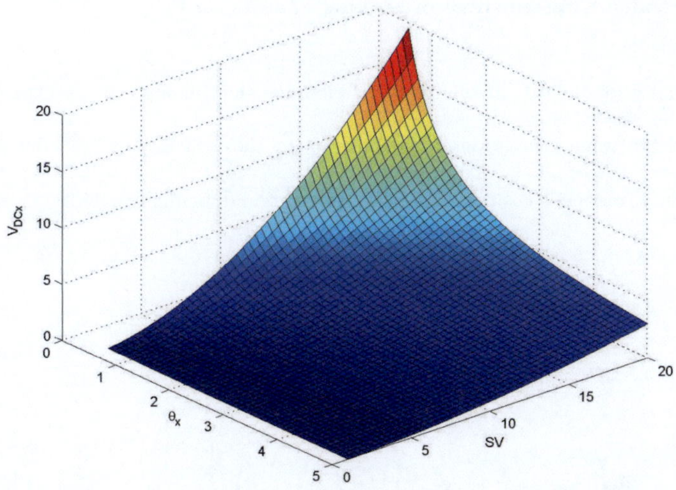

Figure 3.4: The value of the dynamic capability V_{DC_x} as a function of θ_x and SV

in combination with high value generation θ_x ($\theta_x > 4$) lead to an approximately linear

increase of the dynamic capability value V_{DC_x}. However, decreasing value generations θ_x

($\theta_x < 3$), in combination with high salvage values SV ($SV > 15$), lead to exponential

increasing values of the applied dynamic capability to discard capability x.

Based on the results of my simulations concerning the value of a dynamic capability

used to extend a capability, I am able to formulate the following propositions:

PROPOSITION 3.1 *Ceteris paribus, the value of a dynamic capability to discard*

a capability increases in the case of a) a decreasing expected drift rate μ; b) an

increasing market volatility σ; c) an increasing salvage value SV; d) decreasing

prices related to the capability.

3.4.4.2 Value Consequences of Driving Factors on V_{DC_y}

Similar to section 3.4.4.1, in this section I examine the influence of the expected development of the value generation of capability y μ_y, the volatility of the value generation σ_y, and the investment costs qIC on the value of the dynamic capability V_{DC_y} enabling the firm to extend a capability. Inserting the different factors in $V_{DC_y} = B\theta_y^\varepsilon$, I obtain an expression similar to V_{DC_x}:

$$V_{DC_y} \;=\; B\theta_y^\varepsilon \;=\; \cfrac{qIC}{-\frac{1}{2}-\frac{\mu_y}{\sigma_y^2}+\sqrt{\left(\frac{1}{2}-\frac{\mu_y}{\sigma_y^2}\right)^2+\frac{2r}{\sigma_y^2}}}$$

$$\left(qIC\,\frac{r-\mu_y}{c_0(q-1)}\;\cfrac{\frac{1}{2}-\frac{\mu_y}{\sigma_y^2}+\sqrt{\left(\frac{1}{2}-\frac{\mu_y}{\sigma_y^2}\right)^2+\frac{2r}{\sigma_y^2}}}{-\frac{1}{2}-\frac{\mu_x}{\sigma_x^2}+\sqrt{\left(\frac{1}{2}-\frac{\mu_x}{\sigma_x^2}\right)^2+\frac{2r}{\sigma_x^2}}}\,\theta_y^{-1}\right)^{-\left(\frac{1}{2}-\frac{\mu_y}{\sigma_y^2}+\sqrt{\left(\frac{1}{2}-\frac{\mu_y}{\sigma_y^2}\right)^2+\frac{2r}{\sigma_y^2}}\right)}. \tag{3.8}$$

Analogous to analyzing the influence of different parameters on V_{DC_x}, I plot 3-D figures to model the effect of different values of θ_y and one further parameter on V_{DC_y}, while the remaining ones are constant. Based on the simulations providing realistic first passage times, I have chosen the following standard parameters: $\mu_y = 5\%$, $\sigma_y = 25\%$, the extent of the investment by $q = 1.5$, and the investment costs per unit of the capability extension by $IC = 10$. Accordingly, the total investment costs are $qIC = 150$. These standard values lead to $\varepsilon = 1.1177$ and a trigger bound $\bar{\theta}_y$ of 2.8479. The initial value of θ_{y0} is 1. Hence, the following simulations are based on the domain $\theta_y = [\theta_{y0}, \bar{\theta}_y] = [1, 2.8479]$. Again, since $\bar{\theta}_y$ is a function of μ_y, σ_y, and qIC, $\bar{\theta}_y$ represents the value maximizing trigger bound only with regard to the standard values.

Figure 3.5 shows the effects of the actual value generation of capability y in combination with the expected value development μ_y of capability y on the value of the dynamic capability, which the firm applies to enlarge capability y. The domain of μ_y is given by $\mu_y = [4\%, r - 0.001\%] = [4\%, 5.999\%]$. The results indicate, that the assumed value

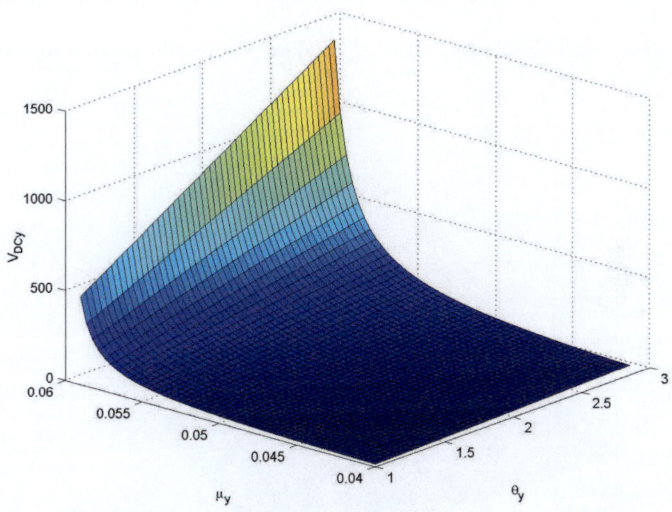

Figure 3.5: The value of the dynamic capability V_{DC_y} as a function of θ_y and μ_y

development of μ_y has got a high impact on the value of dynamic capabilities enabling them to enlarge capabilities. As expected, the highest values of V_{DC_y} are reached by an assumed high growth rate of the value generation of capability y in combination with a high actual value generation of capability y, and whereas, small values of V_{DC_y} in the case of a small assumed capability development in combination with a high actual value generation of capability y. Because of the chosen standard values leading to $\varepsilon = 1.1177$

and the strong influence of μ_y in comparison to θ_y, the increase of the actual capability value θ_y, however, seems to lead to an approximately linear increase of V_{DC_y}, since $\varepsilon > 1$, the development of V_{DC_y} as a function of θ_y follows the curve of a parable. The value μ_y influences rather the degree of the increase.

Figure 3.6 shows the influence of the assumed volatility of the value generation of capability y on V_{DC_y} in combination with θ_y. Indeed, the results indicate that an increase

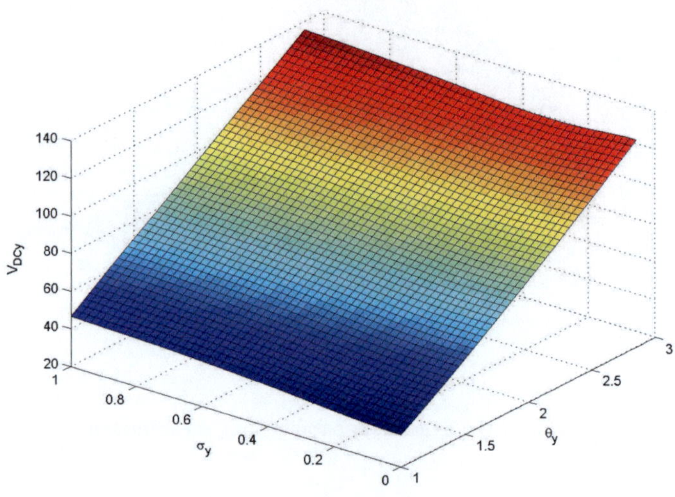

Figure 3.6: The value of the dynamic capability V_{DC_y} as a function of θ_y and σ_y

of the volatility σ_y enhances the value of the dynamic capability, however, compared to an increase of θ_y, the impact of σ_y is by far smaller.

The last simulation (figure 3.7) deals with the consequences of a variation of the investment costs on the dynamic capability value. Since, ceteris paribus, a project becomes

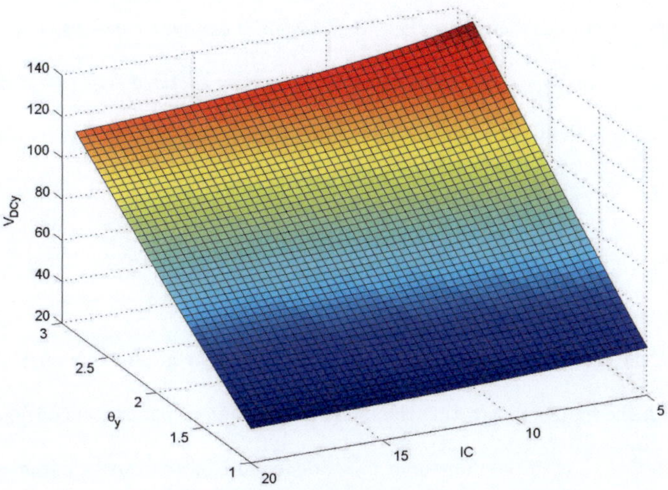

Figure 3.7: The value of the dynamic capability V_{DC_y} as a function of θ_y and IC

more profitable, a decrease of the investment costs leads to higher dynamic capability values. A variation of the investment costs has approximately linear effects on V_{DC_y}, similar to a variation of θ_y. Hence, the highest values of V_{DC_y} are achieved by small investment costs in combination with high values of θ_y. On the other hand the values of V_{DC_y} are small in the case of high investment costs in combination with a small actual value generation of capability y.

Based on the results of my simulations concerning the value of a dynamic capability used to extend a capability, I am able to formulate the following proposition:

PROPOSITION 3.2 *Ceteris paribus, the value of a dynamic capability to extend a capability increases in the case of a) an increasing expected drift rate μ; b) an increasing market volatility σ; c) decreasing investment costs IC; d) increasing prices related to the capability.*

3.4.4.3   A Value Comparison of Dynamic Capabilities

Comparing the figures illustrating the influence of different parameters on V_{DC_x} (figures 3.2-3.4) with the figures illustrating the influence of different parameters on V_{DC_y} (figures 3.5-3.7), I notice that the co-domain of V_{DC_x}, depending on the chosen parameter values, lies inbetween 0 and 20 units, whereas the co-domain of V_{DC_y}, however, depending on other parameter values, is in between approximately 0 and 1300 units.

This result indicates that a dynamic capability used to discard a capability is less worthwhile in comparison to a dynamic capability used to extend a capability. The reason for this result is as follows: the value of a dynamic capability used to discard a capability depends largely on the salvage value SV a firm obtains (cf. equation 3.7).

It might be possible to blow up the value of V_{DC_x} by $\lim \alpha \to 0$, while keeping the remaining parameters constant. However, the interpretation of this constellation is that the firm is able to receive a large salvage value SV by discarding a capability x which generates only small values (cf. equation 3.5). In other words, the ratio of the salvage value to the value generation of a capability has got a huge effect on the value of the dynamic capability used to modify the considered capability.

On the other hand, extending the capability y is accompanied by the known and limited investment costs qIC, in contrast to the value development of the extended capability. This value is exogenously given and might achieve huge values. Therefore, the value of a dynamic capability enabling the firm to extend the considered capability might also achieve huge values.

3.4.5 Absence of Dynamic Capabilities

After examining the value determining factors of dynamic capabilities (cf. sections 3.4.4.1 and 3.4.4.3), I investigate the value consequences caused by the application of dynamic capabilities. To do this, I consider the reference firm already described in the model part (section 3.3). This firm consists of the same resource base and is embedded in the same environment as the firm described above. However, contrary to the previously considered firm (equipped with dynamic capabilities), the newly introduced firm does not possess the ability to change its resource base. The firm's value at any point in time is given by

$$V_{RB}(\theta_x, \theta_y) = \frac{\alpha}{r - \mu_x}\theta_x + \frac{(1 - \alpha)c_0}{r - \mu_y}\theta_y. \tag{3.9}$$

Based on these considerations, I formulate the following proposition:

PROPOSITION 4 *The value difference between a firm optimally using its dynamic capabilities and a firm not adjusting its resource base at all is given by*

$$by$$

$$\Delta V(\theta_x, \theta_y) = \begin{cases} A\theta_x^\gamma + B\theta_y^\varepsilon & : \quad \theta_x > \bar{\theta}_x \wedge \theta_y < \bar{\theta}_y \\[2ex] \frac{qc_0}{r-\mu_y}\theta_y + A\theta_x^\gamma & : \quad \theta_x > \bar{\theta}_x \wedge \theta_y > \bar{\theta}_y \\[2ex] \frac{\alpha c_0}{r-\mu_y}\theta_y + B\theta_y^\varepsilon - \frac{\alpha}{r-\mu_x}\theta_x & : \quad \theta_x < \bar{\theta}_x \wedge \theta_y < \bar{\theta}_y \\[2ex] \frac{(q-1+\alpha)c_0}{r-\mu_y}\theta_y - \frac{\alpha}{r-\mu_x}\theta_x & : \quad \theta_x < \bar{\theta}_x \wedge \theta_y > \bar{\theta}_y. \end{cases} \tag{3.10}$$

Formulating proposition 4, I investigate the value consequences evoked by the existence respectively non-existence of dynamic capabilities.

Another influence factor on the value estimation of a firm is the point in time, when capability changes are executed. Teece (2007) emphasizes the importance for firms to stay flexible, by maintaining different ways of design development, keeping competitors' developments in view, and to invest "heavily in the particular technologies and designs most likely to achieve marketplace acceptance" (Teece 2007, p.1326).

My model does not take competitors' behavior into account, which might be an interesting point to add. However, my approach supports and emphasizes the importance of the chosen point in time to apply a dynamic capability, since it is assumed as being an endogenous variable, and thus can be influenced by the firms' decision makers. Therefore, even though it might be interesting to examine the influence of other parameters on the value consequences that the application of dynamic capabilities have, I focus on the value consequences in the context of time.

3.4.6 Inappropriate Timing of Dynamic Capabilities

To show the value consequence of the absence of dynamic capabilities (cf. section 3.4.5), I introduced a firm possessing dynamic capabilities. However, in this case the firm behaves suboptimal in terms of timing. That is, instead of determining the value maximizing bounds $\bar{\theta}_i$ as triggers to initiate the capability change, the firm arbitrarily chooses a point in time to execute the capability change. Consequently, the capability values $\tilde{\theta}_x$, respectively $\tilde{\theta}_y$, are exogenously given. This assumption leads to the coefficients $\tilde{A}$ and $\tilde{B}$ that are different from A and B:

$$\tilde{A} = SV\tilde{\theta}_x^{-\gamma} - \frac{\alpha}{r - \mu_x}\tilde{\theta}_x^{1-\gamma} \tag{3.11}$$

$$\tilde{B} = \frac{(q-1)c_0}{r - \mu_y}\tilde{\theta}_y^{1-\varepsilon} - qIC\tilde{\theta}_y^{-\varepsilon}. \tag{3.12}$$

Thus, I can formulate proposition 5:

PROPOSITION 5 *Based on my model assumptions, applying its dynamic capabilities suboptimally in terms of time, the firm's value is given by*

$$\tilde{V}(\theta_x, \theta_y) = \begin{cases} \frac{\alpha}{r-\mu_x}\theta_x + \frac{(1-\alpha)c_0}{r-\mu_y}\theta_y + \tilde{A}\theta_x^\gamma + \tilde{B}\theta_y^\varepsilon & : \quad \theta_x > \tilde{\theta}_x \wedge \theta_y < \tilde{\theta}_y \\[2ex] \frac{\alpha}{r-\mu_x}\theta_x + \frac{(1-\alpha)qc_0}{r-\mu_y}\theta_y + \tilde{A}\theta_x^\gamma & : \quad \theta_x > \tilde{\theta}_x \wedge \theta_y > \tilde{\theta}_y \\[2ex] \frac{c_0}{r-\mu_y}\theta_y + \tilde{B}\theta_y^\varepsilon & : \quad \theta_x < \tilde{\theta}_x \wedge \theta_y < \tilde{\theta}_y \\[2ex] \frac{qc_0}{r-\mu_y}\theta_y & : \quad \theta_x < \tilde{\theta}_x \wedge \theta_y > \tilde{\theta}_y. \end{cases} \tag{3.13}$$

The value consequence ΔV is given by

$$\Delta V = V_{Max} - \tilde{V}, \tag{3.14}$$

and differs depending on the firm's optimal capability state and the firm's decision to execute the suboptimal capability change. Figure 3.8 shows the number of different value consequences which may arise due to firm's decisions. $\bar{\theta}_x$ and $\bar{\theta}_y$ indicate the optimal value levels to apply the dynamic capabilities. In the case of $\tilde{\theta}_x^e$, respectively $\tilde{\theta}_y^e$, the firm applied its dynamic capabilities too early, in the case of $\tilde{\theta}_x^l$, respectively $\tilde{\theta}_y^l$, the firm applied the dynamic capability too late. Accordingly, based on the outlined 'two capabilities model', 36 solutions are possible.

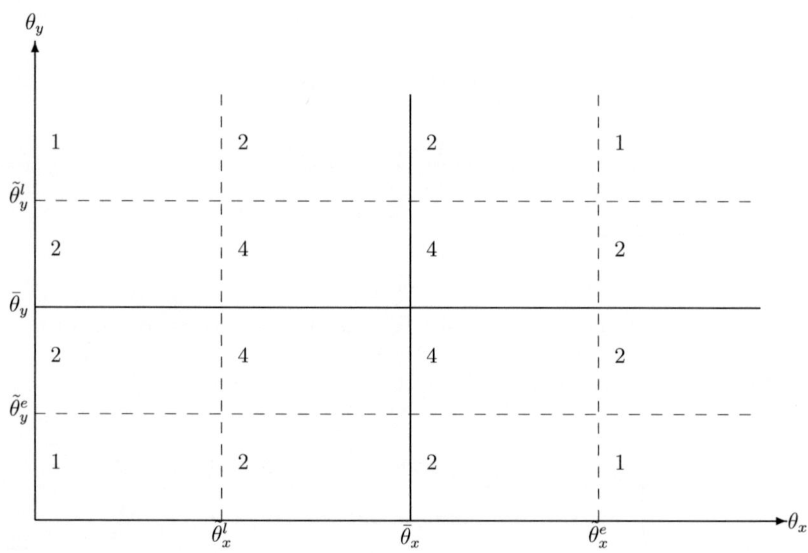

Figure 3.8: Number of solutions with regard to the firm's timing to change capabilities

3.5 Discussions, Limitations & Future Research of the Second Research Objective

The primary aim of this research objective is to investigate the value implications of dynamic capabilities. More concrete, some crucial questions arise if dynamic capabilities are considered from a value perspective: "Do dynamic capabilities generate or do they present value?" "Does the possession of dynamic capabilities and their application have an impact on the firm value?" And: "Is there a value maximizing point in time to apply dynamic capabilities?" If yes: "What are the value consequences of a suboptimal application of dynamic capabilities?".

To answer these research questions, I have developed a mathematical model based on real option knowledge.

I have recognized that the value of a dynamic capability is equal to the value of an option to execute change (cf. Proposition 2). This in mind it can be stated that the firm's value is composed of the accumulated, discounted value generated by the existing resource base *and* the option value to execute modifications of the resource base which is equal to the value of the applied dynamic capability (cf. Proposition 1). Based on the model, I am able to identify the firm's maximal value achieved by optimal resource base adaptation in terms of time, as well as the value consequences of a suboptimal resource base adaptation (cf. Theorem & Proposition 4). Beside the dimension of time, I identify different value driving factors of dynamic capabilities (cf. Proposition 3). These are the predicted value development and volatility of the used capabilities, the investment costs (in the case of capability extension), the salvage value (in the case of capability withdrawal), as well as the current cash flow generation. Assuming that firms act as value maximizer, all factors determining the value of dynamic capabilities are, therefore, externally given. Using 3-D plots of one of these factors in combination with the actual capability value, I am able to identify the impact of these factors on the value of the considered dynamic capability (cf. Propositions 3.1 & 3.2).

The answers of my research questions help researchers to improve their understanding of the nature of dynamic capabilities and the effects of dynamic capabilities on firm value even in an dormant state. Assuming that firms are value maximizers, the propositions 3, 3.1 3.2 indicate that the value of dynamic capabilities depends highly on external factors[1].

With reference to the theorem and proposition 4, I am able to prove Eisenhardt & Martin's (2000) statement, that the long-term competitive advantage lies in "using dynamic capabilities sooner, more astutely, or more fortuitously than the competition to create resource configurations that have that advantage" (Eisenhardt & Martin 2000, p.1117) to be wrong. The application of dynamic capabilities must not imperatively take place sooner or more fortuitously than that carried out by competitors. In contrast, the application of dynamic capabilities should happen at a specific point in time, selected in an astute way.

---

[1]The model is based on the assumption that the dynamic capabilities are time-invariant with regard to their task. (Cf. Zahra et al. (2006))

The results of my research are rather congruent with Teece's (2007) view, to maintain and to improve "technological competences and complementary assets and then, when the opportunity is ripe," to invest "heavily in the particular technologies and designs most likely to achieve marketplace acceptance" (Teece 2007, p.1326).

Besides an increase of academic knowledge, the results of the model have normative implications. For instance, the possession of dynamic capabilities that are able to extend a specific resource base configuration seems to be more valuable than that aligned to discard a resource base configuration (cf. section 3.4.4.3). This justifies the decisions of managers to make more effort to develop dynamic capabilities that are trained to extend existing resource base configurations instead of those used to abandon resource base reconfigurations. Additionally, the simulations indicate that the velocity of market change has a higher impact on the value of dynamic capabilities than the market volatility (cf. 3.2, 3.3, and 3.5, 3.6). Therefore, managers should rather focus on the expected market development than on market volatility.

However, my simulations are based on selected values, respectively on specific domains and absolute values. To further follow this research avenue, the next step should be to investigate the impact of the identified driving factors on the value of dynamic capabilities in ratio to each other. Likewise, it would be interesting to analyze the impact of dynamic capabilities on firm value in relation to the value generation of the capabilities in place. This approach should also contain an investigation of the influence of different driving factors on the ratio of dynamic capability value to firm value.

A further near at hand step in research is to verify the model or adaptations of this model by the use of quantitative data. In this case, the dependent variable is the value of dynamic capabilities. However, even though the value of the firm is known (e.g the stock value) a split of this value into the value of dynamic capabilities and the value of the resources in place is, to the best of my knowledge, not possible. Therefore, in the case of known values of the parameters used in my model, the value of the resources in place and the value of the dynamic capabilities can be - on the condition that the model is well adapted to reality - calculated and compared with the firm's value, while a comparison of the calculated dynamic capability value and the given dynamic capability value is not be possible.

Despite this hindrance an empirical verification of my model might be possible. Indeed, I am convinced that the outlined model is suitable to explain the existence of management consultancies, and their intensive deployment in times of economic boom or slowdown: Similar to Teece (2007), who emphasizes the importance of promoters and visionaries to overcome 'naysayers' in order to realize internal views and execute necessary resource base changes, Eisenhardt & Martin (2000) refer to 'heavyweight' team leaders to allow an effective application of dynamic capabilities. On the same subject, Adner & Helfat (2003) demonstrate that the decisions of firm managers that lead to an heterogeneity of firms' resources, even if these firms operate in the same industry, depend largely on 'managerial' dynamic capabilities. In other words, different resource bases of firms develope, because of the fact that managers are equipped with different managerial and social capacities, as well as different managerial cognition. To summarize, the effectiveness and efficiency of dynamic capabilities seem to depend largely on the intellectual and social capabilities of managers, promoters, visionaries, or 'heavyweight' team leaders.

Adding Winter's (2003) insights, that the development of sophisticated dynamic capabilities is linked to costs and, therefore, may have negative effects on firm performance, or even may disturb the value creation of well-functioning capabilities (Zahra et al. 2006), an 'out-sourcing' of dynamic capabilities seems - under specific conditions - to be the best alternative. As the result of this out-sourcing process, management consultancies, whose core competences are to help firms to adapt their resource bases, have come into existence. In this context it is essential to hone the contact to selected management consultancies to ensure the application of the "out-sourced" dynamic capabilities at the value maximizing point in time and finally to keep the value high.

In contrast to firms consisting of a value generating resource base *and* dynamic capabilities, management consultancies founded to support firms to realize resource base changes represent "pure" dynamic capabilities. Thus, with regard to management consultancies, the value of dynamic capabilities can empirically be measured[2]. Therefore, based on my model and my simulations, I am able to predict, respectively verify based on sales data of consultancies the correctness of my model.

More concrete, with regard to proposition 3, 3.1 & 3.2 my model is suitable to predict the workload of management consultancies, or, vice versa, the workload of management consultancies is suitable to verify my model. The reason for this statement is

---

[2]With regard to firms comprising value generating resources and dynamic capabilities a comparison of the calculated dynamic capability value and the *real* dynamic capability value of the firm is not possible (cf. Theorem; equation with two unknowns).

as follows: In times of predictable and slow environment changes, firms are rather not interested in changing their resource bases, since they are well-adapted to their external environment (cf. sections 3.4.4.1 and 3.4.4.3, in particular figures 3.2 and 3.5). In fact, they attempt to avoid costs and, therefore, neglect the development of dynamic capabilities. However, in times of changing environments, dynamic capabilities are needed to adapt the resource base to environmental shifts. To achieve a rapid and well-thought-out resource base adaptation, based on 'best practice' (Eisenhardt & Martin 2000), firms engage management consultancies. Following these insights, the revenues of management consultancies generated in these markets should be significantly higher than the revenues generated in moderately changing markets.

In addition, also based on the results of the outlined model, the revenues should be significantly higher in markets, in which high value generating capabilities are employed, in comparison to markets equipped with low value generating capabilities (cf. sections 3.4.4.1 and 3.4.4.3). The further driving factors of dynamic capability value might also be a subject of investigations.

Another research approach, based on the outlined model, might be to improve managers' decisions with regard to resource base modification: changes of the resource base are often aimed at one direction only and are irreversible, and, therefore, should not only be a matter of value maximization. A firm's managers should - in particular if the firm operates in highly changing environments - also consider the risk a firm faces due to changes in its resource base. The outlined model and the executed calculations are suitable to estimate the firm's risk of changes, which results from the abandonment or the extension of an existing capability.

In chapter 3, my research is organized to provide answers to theoretical implications in the context of the value of dynamic capabilities. The contents of chapter 4 are in contrast of crucial normative relevance. Researchers define the challenge to firms operating in innovative markets in order to improve existing products, technologies, or even capabilities, and at the same time to develop completely new products, technologies, and capabilities as ambidexterity. These firms are often confronted with the challenge to find the right balance between exploration and exploitation, respectively the value maximizing point in time to exploit one product and to introduce a new product into a prospering market. In the following chapter I present a formal model based on insights of real option theory to determine in a one-firm model the value maximizing point in time.

Chapter 4

Third Research Objective: Optimal Timing of Resource Base Adaptation*

Firms operating in changing environments are often forced to follow at least two strategies simultaneously: First, to improve the existing products accompanied by incremental process advances to ensure the current cash flows. Second, ensure future cash flows, to develop new technologies, processes, and products, to create, or to be able to follow standards of new markets. In research the first task is described as exploitation, the second as exploration. The concept of integrating the contradicting requirements arising from these activities is called 'ambidexterity'. A basic challenge of ambidextrous firms is to orchestrate the resource allocation to accomplish an optimal balance of exploitation and exploration with regard to external shifts. In this chapter, starting from a firm continuously improving and selling a product in a declining market (exploitation) and building or fostering the option to launch a product into an emerging market (exploration), I present a formal approach suitable to deduce the optimal balance of exploitation and exploration. Using profit maximization as the target dimension, assuming that the future cash flows of product selling are exogenously given and of limited prediction, I refer to real option insights to demonstrate that there exist defined points in time until when to maintain, taper off or stress and finally stop exploitative and explorative activities. Since I deal with stochastic processes, these points in time can only be determined in real time. Therefore, I further develop my model to enable the prediction of the value maximizing point in time depending on the value realizations of the influence factors.

*I would like to thank Prof. Dr. Baldauf and Prof. Dr. Dockner for their valuable suggestions and constructive proposals which they made during the phases of model construction and implementation.

4.1 Introduction to the Third Research Objective

Firms operating worldwide are faced with an increasing rate of innovation and change. This forces them to develop a flexible resource base as well as strategic concepts delivering the ability to react to threats and opportunities (Teece 2007). The most comprehensive approach developed to identify the requirements of firms to stay flexible is the dynamic capability concept (Teece et al. 1997, Eisenhardt & Martin 2000, Winter 2003, Teece 2007). Dynamic capabilities provide a firm with the capacity to "purposefully create, extend, or modify its resource base" (Helfat et al. 2007, p.4), in order to achieve and maintain competitive advantage in the long-run (cf. chapter 2 and 3).

In contrast to the dynamic capability concept the concept of ambidexterity focuses on firms aiming to achieve short- and long-term competitiveness via efficiency and innovation by simultaneously engaging in exploitation and exploration (Duncan 1976, March 1991, Tushman & O'Reilly 1996, O'Reilly & Tushman 2007). Exploitation means to operate in markets including the improvement of existing technologies and processes, as long as they are profitable. Exploration means to develop new products, firm inherent processes or technologies that are distinct from existing ones for existing or emerging markets (March 1991).

Similar to firms possessing dynamic capabilities, firms that behave in an ambidextrous way must possess the capacity to orchestrate their resources by means of a complex set of routines and processes to ensure a balanced ratio of exploration and exploitation with regard to external environment shifts (O'Reilly & Tushman 2007). This implies the ability of the firm's management to handle conflicts concerning intra-organizational resource allocation. Since these research issues are objects of the dynamic capability and ambidexterity research, O'Reilly & Tushman (2007) view the firm's ability to behave 'ambidextrously' as a dynamic capability.

However, the basic problem of ambidextrous firms is to identify and to achieve the optimal balance of exploitative activities to follow the developments of existing markets and explorative activities to develop or to be prepared for arising markets (March 1991, Adler, Goldoftas & Levine 1999, Brown & Duguid 2001, Katila & Ahuja 2002, O'Reilly & Tushman 2007). To apply too much of a firm's limited resources on exploitative activities means to imperil the development of future technologies, processes, and products (March 1991, Benner & Tushman 2002). A further threat is to lose the ability to follow disruptive environment changes (Hannan & Freeman 1984), because of an increase of 'inertia' or the loss of the capacity to absorb, to understand, and to integrate essential information (Cohen & Levinthal 1990). A disproportional shift of a firm's resources towards explorative activities leads to losing contact to markets which ensure the "earning-now", an atrophy of core competence as well as an increase of development costs of perhaps hard to manufacture, hard to sell or even over-engineered products (March 1991).

In the following I assume that the optimal balance of exploitative and explorative activities of a firm depends largely on the maturity of current and future markets (Tushman & Romanelli 1985, Burgelman 1991, Tushman & O'Reilly 1996). For instance, a firm operating in a prospering market while a rise of a new market that neither imperils nor provides any opportunities is not perceptible, is well advised to deploy a major part of its resources on exploitative activities. In contrast, a firm operating in a stagnating or even decreasing market that is additionally imperiled by an increasing market should shift its resources from exploitative activities towards explorative activities. In such a situation there exists a certain danger that the behavior of firms is similar to that of the proverbial 'boiling frog'. Instead of shifting resources to prepare the change towards new technologies or products in advance[1], they focus on the improvement of existing products until it is too late[2].

To achieve an optimal balance of exploitative activities and explorative activities with regard to environmental shifts firms are faced with two central challenges: First to *determine* the optimal point in time when to discard a specific exploitative activity (e.g. withdrawal of a product from a declining market) and when to stress explorative activities (e.g. introduction of a new product into an emerging market). Second to *predict* the optimal point in time to discard exploitative activities and to stress explorative activities in order to ensure the optimal balance of explorative and exploitative activities along the time-line.

An open question in this line of reasoning is what the optimal point in time is when to discard a specific exploitative activity and to focus more on an explorative activity. Since firms in the private industry are profit maximizers, an appropriate target dimension obviously presents the firms' profits. Accordingly, the optimal points in time to discard

---

[1]To prepare the frog's jump out of the water at the optimal point of time
[2]The frog's adapting to the temperature of the water

a specific exploitative activity and to stress an explorative activity are those that lead to the maximization of the firms' profits.

With regard to these concepts and assumptions, I introduce a formal model to investigate the optimal behavior of ambidextrous organizations referring directly to the supervision of their product portfolio and indirectly to the appropriate balance of their explorative and exploitative activities.

The model has been developed under the premises of being best applicable to large companies operating in fields characterized by high innovation rates. The considered firms are active in different markets, each market offering a variety of products. To ensure long term survival, these firms are challenged to develop and to launch new products simultaneously.

Because of considerations of simplicity, I reduce the multi-product portfolio of a firm to two products, one exploiting a declining market efficiently, the other being at a stage of the life-cycle when it could be launched into an emerging market. I assume that the cash flow stream generated by the products sold in the declining market is partly predictable, but decreasing. Consequently, the firm will be confronted with the challenge of taking the product from the market and of executing a divestment process releasing a salvage value, in other words to discard an exploitative activity. Referring to the emerging market the firm is faced with the opportunity to have a share of a presumably increasing but unpredictable cash flow. Since market development and product standards are uncertain, the firm retains investments in production facilities, marketing, sales person education, etc., even though the prototype has already reached a market ripe level from the technological point of view. In this situation, the firm still retains explorative activities. However, as soon as the potential cash flow stream reaches a level that justifies investments, the firm is advised to spend the needed amount to enter the market. In this situation a resource shift to support explorative activities is necessary.

To ascertain that the firm generates a continuous cash flow stream by selling products the firm accepts only those investment costs and salvage values that ensure its presence either in declining or emerging markets, or both. Based on this assumption, I can infer the following situations: the starting point is given by the firm selling a product in the declining market only, followed by a phase of selling products in the declining and emerging markets. The final state is characterized by the firm selling only the new product in the emerging market. However, theoretically, there might also occur a situation when the points in time to exit the declining and to enter the emerging markets coincide.

Both decisions, either to exit the declining market, or to launch the product into the emerging market, represent options. As I assume that both cash flow streams are exogenously given, the real option theory provides an appropriate instrument to determine the optimal timing and to identify important influence factors. However, this model only provides the optimal point in time to withdraw the sold product from the declining market and to launch the new product into the emerging market in real time. Indeed, a prediction of the optimal points in time is possible.

To summarize, based on my model a firm is able to determine and to predict the profit maximizing point in time until which an exploitative activity should last (exploiting a declining market) and to determine and to predict the profit maximizing point in time at which an explorative activity should be finished (the preparation of the entry in an emerging market).

Apart from the academic implication to provide an answer to a fundamental question in ambidextrous research, namely to find the optimal ratio of exploitation and exploration and to understand the main influence factors (March 1991), my model also provides normative implications. Using an adapted model the firm's decision makers possess an instrument supporting them when aiming at an optimal balance of explorative and exploitative activities.

The remainder of this article is organized as followed: Since the model is directly based on the ambidextrous concept, in section 4.2, I review relevant research literature with regard to ambidexterity. In section 4.3, I introduce the model assumptions and the mathematical specifications. Section 4.4 represents the results and the main proposition, examined and clarified by simulations. In the last section of this chapter I discuss the findings, show limitations and outline future research possibilities.

4.2 Ambidexterity

To ignore that the incremental improvement of existing products may lead to a decrease of the current cash flow, whereas, to ignore disruptive developments of new technologies may lead to missing future markets, and may additionally represent platforms to 'attack' existing markets. Therefore, to remain competitive, companies operating in fields characterized by high innovation rates should not only improve their existing products and processes, but should also develop new products and processes (Tushman & O'Reilly 1996, Birkinshaw & Gibson 2004, He & Wong 2004, O'Reilly & Tushman 2004).

The ability of a firm to execute incremental improvements referred to as exploitation, and the ability to successfully execute and follow disruptive technology changes represents exploration (March 1991). Both abilities are characterized by requirements which are diametrically opposite in their orientation.

Exploitation consists of elements like refinement, efficiency, and variance reduction (O'Reilly & Tushman 2007), as well as of focusing on existing products and processes (Smith & Tushman 2005). In contrast, exploration consists of variation and flexibility (March 1991). Contrary to the starting point of exploitation as modification of existing processes or products by the frequent use of established routines, enhanced by further development of internal or the absorption of external knowledge, the starting point of exploration is rather calling the existing products and processes in question, focusing on the basic challenges the firm's core competencies are aligned to, and trying to find solutions using the firm's capacity to create new approaches (Levinthal & March 1993, Baum, Xiao Li & Usher 2000, Danneels 2000, Kyriakopoulos & Moorman 2004). Hence, the expected outcomes of exploitative efforts are close to the existing technologies, and consequently - mostly - positive and predictable, contrary to explorative efforts, which are indeed 'distant' from existing technologies, and as a result are coupled with risk and uncertainty, and therefore linked with higher failure-rates (March 1991).

Considering these contradictory requirements, the challenge to integrate both approaches becomes self-evident (Dougherty & Hardy 1996, Benner & Tushman 2003, He & Wong 2004). Firms often drift involuntarily to either exploration or exploitation (Benner & Tushman 2002). Being too exploitative, firms frequently avoid explorative attempts, which impede the development of innovative products and additionally strengthen exploitative ways of thinking (March 1991, Benner & Tushman 2002, Burgelman 2002). Being too exploitative may also lead to an insufficient capacity of adapting efficiently and effectively to disruptive environments (Hannan & Freeman 1984), not only because of 'inertia', but also because of an underdeveloped ability to absorb, filter, and integrate new and external information (Cohen & Levinthal 1990). In contrast, focussing too much on exploration may lead to neglecting the earning-now, while at the same time it entails costs of experimentation, over-engineering of products, development of products characterized by high manufacturing costs as well as dwindling of core competence (March 1991, Burgelman 2002).

Since the consequences of an unbalanced innovation strategy are far reaching, the main issue in this context is to find the optimal ratio between explorative and exploitative endeavors. In general, researchers assume that a disposition towards exploitation in rather stable markets leads to higher performances, while shifting the ratio between exploitation and exploration towards exploration leads to higher performances in high velocity environments.

However, these findings do not reflect all the aspects arising from the complexity of this topic. An increasing number of studies examines the ambidexterity approach from different perspectives (He & Wong 2004, Smith & Tushman 2005, Jansen, Van Den Bosch & Volberda 2005, Gupta, Smith & Shalley 2006, March 2006, O'Reilly & Tushman 2007). The main focus is on how firms can handle incremental and revolutionary changes simultaneously in order to ensure stable firm conditions across product life-cycles (Tushman & O'Reilly 1996).

In this context, Tushman & O'Reilly (1996) emphasize the importance of organization structures to support both innovation strategies simultaneously. Even though the units are separated by differences in culture and processes, they should be aligned to exploit their strengths depending on the external situation.

On the same subject, O'Reilly & Tushman (2004) propose to link the units on the corporate level in such a manner that firms are able to use resources both sided. In this case, mutual benefits arise because of knowledge transfer, while at the same time the peril of negative interventions caused by interactions between the units is avoided. Similar concepts are expressed by Markides & Charitou (2004) and Jansen et al. (2005).

A different perspective linked to the single-employee-level is given by Gibson & Birkinshaw (2004) who stress that beyond a firm's structure the combination of stretch, discipline, support, and trust are essential elements to facilitate ambidextrous behavior.

O'Reilly & Tushman's (2007) approach to conceive ambidexterity as a specification of a dynamic capability is central to the development of our theoretical foundations:

O'Reilly & Tushman (2007) define ambidexterity as the firm's ability to recognize threats and opportunities and reconfigure the resource base appropriately, so as to avoid being trapped into an ineffective situation because of path dependency. These demands, fulfilled by activities of exploitation and exploration, reflect the basic ideas that researchers have concerning ambidextrous organizations. However, O'Reilly & Tushman's (2007) approach is more comprehensive compared to those of Tushman & O'Reilly (1996) or Gibson & Birkinshaw (2004). To fully utilize the firm's abilities of exploitation and exploration, it is insufficient to employ concepts referring only to the individual level or to emphasize the importance of implementation of an appropriate organization structure. The firm must rather systematically conceptualize, apply, and re-conceptualize approaches in order to maintain such important dimensions as processes, culture, leadership qualities, and adaptable strategies. Since the model focuses on the optimal timing regarding product introduction and abandonment, which implies the ability to coordinate valuable resources, I, in particular, follow O'Reilly & Tushman's (2007) understanding of ambidexterity.

4.3 Model Description

4.3.1 Model Rationales

The developed model reflects and examines the basic idea of ambidextrous behavior in terms of time. Reduced to its fundamentals, ambidexterity consists of the firm's ability to execute the two actions of exploitation and exploration. Exploitation is characterized by using existing conditions efficiently, while exploration is characterized by actions of a disruptive nature (respectively by preparing actions of a disruptive nature). In the value chain context, selling products efficiently in declining or emerging markets can be interpreted as an exploitative action, while the abandonment, but in particular the introduction of a product, accompanied by investment strategies, can be seen as an explorative activity (O'Reilly & Tushman 2007).

The reasons why firms decide to exit markets or to introduce new products to existing or emerging markets may vary. However, such actions are strongly influenced by market conditions which arise over time. For example, the abandonment of a product becomes an option if a firm actively selling products in declining markets recognizes that the expected and discounted cash flow rate undercuts some specific value. Such decisions are linked with an alteration of the producing resources, including salvage values the firm obtains by selling the applied resources.

Similarly, the introduction of a new product in an emerging market becomes a topic of interest, if the expected cash flow crosses a boundary depending on investment costs the firm has to raise. While the abandonment of a product may occur at any time, the introduction of a new product may happen or not. In the first case, it is a question of *'when?'*, in the second case a question of *'when?'* and *'what?'*.

Reducing the research issue to the questions of when and what, the problem fits into Teece's (2007) description of challenges associated with dynamic capabilities: "Staying flexible until the dominant design emerges and then investing heavily once a design looks like it can become the winner" (Teece 2007, p.1326) describes the essence of my research issue.

By focusing on the ability to exploit a declining market efficiently and at the same time to observe market conditions, detect, and seize opportunities, I investigate the basic characteristics of ambidextrous behavior (Tushman & O'Reilly 1996, Birkinshaw & Gibson 2004, He & Wong 2004, O'Reilly & Tushman 2007). With regard to timing, I am aware that finding out the right moment is not enough to introduce products successfully, or to remove products from existing markets. It is rather a question of resource allocation, business models, organizational structure, fitting products, etc. (O'Reilly & Tushman 2007, Teece 2007). Therefore, even though the model conceptualizes ambidexterity, it is simultaneously functioning as a link to support O'Reilly & Tushman's (2007) conception of ambidexterity as a dynamic capability, defining ambidexterity as an ability to possess routines required to manage the complex requirements of product introduction, and abandonment while exploiting existing markets efficiently.

4.3.2   Model Assumptions

The basics of my model are as followed: I consider a firm actively selling a product in a declining market and with the option to exit. Additionally, I assume that the considered firm has completed or will soon complete the development of a prototype and, therefore, possesses the option to enter an emerging market.

Obviously, the validity of my model is restricted to companies which are able to execute exploitation and exploration at the same time. Since, following simultaneously both strategies requires the existence of a certain resource base size and, furthermore, is linked to risk of failure not only with regard to R&D, but also with regard to product introduction, the outline of my model fits to firms that cross a certain boundary in order to provide the necessary resource base and to bolster, if necessary, unsuccessful projects. Accordingly, small and medium sized companies are often more successful when focussing on one strategy only (Ebben & Johnson 2005). Nevertheless, I assume that the company size of the considered firms does not reach a level enabling them to influence significantly market conditions.

Furthermore, the market is characterized by a high degree of competition, coupled with a high rate of innovation. This assumption is consistent with the generally accepted idea that ambidextrous behavior of firms is associated with dynamic environments (Lee, Lee & Lee 2003, Siggelkow & Levinthal 2003, Jansen et al. 2005, Siggelkow & Rivkin 2006). In such markets, the average change of sales volumes, revenues, and cash flows per time unit can be assumed to be higher in comparison to more moderate markets with a smaller number of rivals. However, the dynamics of markets go hand in hand with uncertainty. Therefore, even though an approximate forecasting of revenues, sales volumes, or cash flows is feasible, the exact numbers are subject to a certain volatility. Since I suggest a profit maximizing behavior of firms, the considered firm exploits markets efficiently, independently operating in declining or emerging markets.

To exit declining markets releases resources reflected by a salvage value, contrary to the introduction of new products which can only take place by investments. Since the considered firm operates in markets characterized by high innovation rates, the applied resource base to produce the products sold in the declining market becomes obsolete in short time. Therefore, I can assume that the salvage value the firm achieves, when it exits a declining market, is small compared to the predicted future revenues. Further, the investment costs to introduce the new product are low, compared to the expected present value of future cash flows. Both assumptions explain short product life-cycles of the markets I focus on, in comparison to high investment industries (e.g. aerospace, military industry, shipbuilding, investments in oil industry (e.g offshore)).

4.3.3 Mathematical Specifications

I consider a firm actively selling the product x in a declining market with the option to exit. In case the option is exercised, the firm receives the salvage value SV. Additionally, the firm possesses the option to enter an emerging market by launching product y. However, this product introduction is accompanied by the investment costs IC. The cash flows generated by selling the products x and y are derived from two exogenous price processes denoted θ_x and θ_y, that follow a Geometric Brownian Motion (GBM):

$$d\theta_x(t) \;=\; \mu_x\theta_x(t)dt + \sigma_x\theta_x(t)dW_x(t) \tag{4.1}$$

$$d\theta_y(t) \;=\; \mu_y\theta_y(t)dt + \sigma_y\theta_y(t)dW_y(t). \tag{4.2}$$

The parameters μ_i describe the time-invariant growth rate, σ_i the time-invariant cash flow volatilities, and $dW_i(t) \sim N(0,1)$ the Wiener increments of the stochastic processes $\theta_i(t)$, $i = x, y$. The parameter $\theta_x(t)$ describes the cash flow process related to product x, such as $\theta_y(t)$ to y. Since future cash flows earned through the application of the capabilities x and y are less valuable for the firm, I use the risk less interest rate r $(r > 0)$ to discount the in the future earned cash flows. The declining market is characterized by a negative growth rate ($\mu_x < 0$), and the emerging market by average increasing expected cash flows ($\mu_y > 0$). To ensure the resolvability of the model, I am furthermore forced to assume $\mu_y < r$.

The starting point of my model is the firm selling only product x. Triggered by a certain cash flow level, the firm decides to invest IC, and launches product y into the emerging market. In the case of a cash flow reaching a specific level the firm's decision makers are induced to exit the declining market in favor of the salvage value SV.

Considering these process steps, the firm is faced with the decision problem to detect and determine the optimal points in time to enter the emerging market (τ_1) and to exit the declining market (τ_2). In other words, the firm strives to maximize the accumulated with r discounted expected cash flow V described by the objective function 4.3:

$$
\begin{aligned}
V(\theta_x, \theta_y) &= \max_{\tau_1, \tau_2} E \left\{ \int_0^{\tau_1} c_x \theta_x e^{-rt} dt - ICe^{-\tau_1 r} + \int_{\tau_1}^{\tau_2} [c_x \theta_x + c_y \theta_y] e^{-r(t-\tau_1)} + SVe^{-\tau_2 r} dt \right. \\
&\quad \left. + \int_{\tau_2}^{\infty} c_y \theta_y e^{-r(t-\tau_2)} dt \right\}.
\end{aligned}
\tag{4.3}
$$

Applying stochastic processes, I use the operator $E\{\cdot\}$ to calculate the expected cash flow V. The parameters c_x and c_y describe the intensity with which the firm exploits two markets efficiently.

Following a standard real options approach, the optimal exercise date τ_1 is defined as the first passage when the process $\theta_x(t)$ hits the threshold level $\bar{\theta}_x$. Alternatively, the date τ_2 is defined as the first passage when the process $\theta_y(t)$ hits the threshold $\bar{\theta}_y$. The choice of the two threshold levels is endogenous and driven by the properties of the cash flow processes $\theta_x(t)$ and $\theta_y(t)$, the salvage value SV, and the investment costs IC. Although I cannot predict the values of τ_1 and τ_2, but to adhere to the model framework, I choose the values of SV and IC so that the firm exits the declining market after entering the emerging market.

4.4 Product Introduction & Withdrawal

4.4.1 Value Maximizing Timing

Based on the solution of the firm's decision problem to determine the optimal points in time to introduce product y and to abandon the production of product x (equation 4.3), the following theorem is formulated:

THEOREM 1 *Under the assumptions that the firm is able to determine optimally the point in time to introduce a product to an emerging market, and to
withdraw a product from a declining market, the expected discounted profit is
a function of θ_x and θ_y and is given by*

$$
V(\theta_x, \theta_y) = \begin{cases} \frac{c_x}{r-\mu_x}\theta_x + A\theta_x^\gamma + B\theta_y^\varepsilon & : \quad \theta_x > \bar{\theta}_x \wedge \theta_y < \bar{\theta}_y \\[2mm] \frac{c_x}{r-\mu_x}\theta_x + \frac{c_y}{r-\mu_y}\theta_y + A\theta_x^\gamma & : \quad \theta_x > \bar{\theta}_x \wedge \theta_y > \bar{\theta}_y \\[2mm] \frac{c_y}{r-\mu_y}\theta_y & : \quad \theta_x < \bar{\theta}_x \wedge \theta_y > \bar{\theta}_y, \end{cases} \tag{4.4}
$$

with

$$
A = \frac{c_x \bar{\theta}_x}{\gamma(\mu_x - r)} \bar{\theta}_x^{-\gamma} \quad ; \quad \gamma = \frac{1}{2} - \frac{\mu_x}{\sigma_x^2} - \sqrt{\left(\frac{1}{2} - \frac{\mu_x}{\sigma_x^2}\right)^2 + \frac{2r}{\sigma_x^2}} \quad ; \quad \bar{\theta}_x = \frac{\gamma}{\gamma - 1} \frac{r - \mu_x}{c_x} SV
$$

$$
B = \frac{c_y \bar{\theta}_y}{\varepsilon(r - \mu_y)} \bar{\theta}_y^{-\varepsilon} \quad ; \quad \varepsilon = \frac{1}{2} - \frac{\mu_y}{\sigma_y^2} + \sqrt{\left(\frac{1}{2} - \frac{\mu_y}{\sigma_y^2}\right)^2 + \frac{2r}{\sigma_y^2}} \quad ; \quad \bar{\theta}_y = \frac{\varepsilon}{\varepsilon - 1} \frac{r - \mu_y}{c_y} IC.
$$

$$(4.5)$$

PROOF Cf. appendix B.

The terms $\frac{c_x}{r-\mu_x}\theta_x$ and $\frac{c_y}{r-\mu_y}\theta_y$ reflect the accumulated expected and with r discounted future cash flows generated by the sale of product x and product y. The option value to stop selling product x for the benefits of the salvage value SV is given by $A\theta_x^\gamma$, the option value to enter the emerging market is linked with the investment costs IC, given by $B\theta_y^\varepsilon$.

As mentioned above, a crucial aspect of ambidextrous behavior is to orchestrate resources deliberately and in advance to avoid conflicts due to resource limitations or inappropriate allocation. Accordingly, the firm's ability to predict the optimal point in time to introduce or withdraw products will reduce costs and will enhance project success, since the firm's management is able to plan and coordinate appropriate actions in advance.

4.4.2 Forecasting the Profit Maximizing Point in Time $E\{T\}$

The optimal point in time to introduce the product y or withdraw the product x is determined by the point in time the actual cash flow θ_i, generated by the products, reaches the trigger bound $\bar{\theta}_i$ for the first time. As far as I model the exogenously given cash flow streams by stochastic processes, the accurate point in time at which the product introduction or withdrawal should take place, can only be determined in real time ($\theta_i = \bar{\theta}_i$). However, based on the following theorem, I am able to predict the *expected* point in time when a product introduction, respectively a product withdrawal leads to cash flow maximization.

THEOREM 2 *Under the assumption that the firm follows an expected profit maximizing strategy, the firm is able to predict the expected point in time $E\{T_i\}$, $(i = x, y)$ to withdraw a product x from a declining market and to introduce a product y to an emerging market y by the use of the following equations*

$$E\{T_x\} = \frac{\ln\frac{\bar{\theta}_x}{\theta_x}}{\mu_x - \frac{1}{2}\sigma_x^2} - \frac{\frac{1}{2}\sigma_x^2}{\left(\mu_x - \frac{1}{2}\sigma_x^2\right)^2}\left[1 - \left(\frac{\bar{\theta}_x}{\theta_x}\right)^{\left(1 - \frac{2\mu_x}{\sigma_x^2}\right)}\right] \tag{4.6}$$

$$E\{T_y\} = \frac{\ln\frac{\bar{\theta}_y}{\theta_y}}{\mu_y - \frac{1}{2}\sigma_y^2} - \frac{\frac{1}{2}\sigma_y^2}{\left(\mu_y - \frac{1}{2}\sigma_y^2\right)^2}\left[1 - \left(\frac{\bar{\theta}_y}{\theta_y}\right)^{\left(1 - \frac{2\mu_y}{\sigma_y^2}\right)}\right]. \tag{4.7}$$

PROOF Cf. Song (2001).

$E\{T_x\}$ describes the expected optimal point in time to withdraw product x from the declining market, and $E\{T_y\}$ the expected optimal point in time to introduce product y to the emerging market.

4.4.2.1 Effects of Market Factors on $E\{T_x\}$: Product Withdrawal

The easiest and most efficient way to show clearly the effects of the predicted cash flow development μ_i, the cash flow volatility σ_i, the salvage value SV and the investment costs IC on $E\{T_i\}$, is to vary one parameter, while the remaining parameters rest constant. Since the current cash flow stream θ_x, respectively the assumed cash flow stream θ_y, generated by selling the products x and y are the only time variant parameters, I generate

3-D figures comprising a variation of θ_i, one further parameter and the expected first passage time $E\{T_i\}$.

With regard to $E\{T_x\}$ the standard values of the following simulations are $r = 0.06$, $\mu_x = -0.05$, $\sigma_x = 0.15$, $\alpha = 0.9$, $c_x = 1$. The domain of one of these parameters is given by $\Phi_x \in [\Phi_x^b, \Phi_x^s]$; $\Phi_x = \mu_x, \sigma_x, IC$. Since I am interested in the combination of θ_x and Φ_x leading to $E\{T_x\} = 0$, the domain of θ_x is determined by the starting point θ_{x0} and the bound $\bar{\theta}_x^s$ ($\theta_x \in [\bar{\theta}_x^s; \theta_{x0}]$). $\bar{\theta}_x^s$ is defined as the greatest bound ($\bar{\theta}_x^s = \max\{\bar{\theta}_x(\Phi_x)\}$).

However, $\bar{\theta}_x^s$ does not describe the value maximizing bound $\bar{\theta}_x$ for all Φ_x, but only for Φ_x^s. Therefore, $E\{T_x\}$ only reaches 0 in the case of θ_x approaching $\bar{\theta}_x^s$ under the condition of Φ_x^s. In the case of $\Phi_x \neq \Phi_x^s$ $E\{T_x\} > 0$. To sum up, $E\{T_x\}$ only becomes zero under the condition of $\Phi_x = \Phi_x^s$ and $\theta_x = \bar{\theta}_x^s$. As far as $\bar{\theta}_x^s$ is a function of μ_x, σ_x, and IC, $\bar{\theta}_x^s$ must be calculated anew for each simulation. Examining the following figures, the reader will understand these considerations.

Figure 4.1 is based on the domains $\theta_x \in [0.5423; 5]$ and $\mu_x \in [-0.1, -0.01]$. θ_x approaching $\bar{\theta}_x^s$ the expected first passage time $E\{T_x\}$ converges 0 almost independently on the assumed cash flow development μ_x. In the case of small values of μ_x ($\mu_x < -0.08$), the influence of θ_x on $E\{T_x\}$ is strongly damped, contrary to μ_x taking higher values.

Figure 4.2 shows the development of $E\{T_x\}$ depending on the actual cash flow θ_x and the cash flow volatility σ_x. The chosen domains are $\theta_x \in [0.6600, 5]$ and $\sigma_x \in [0.01, 0.25]$. Similar to figure 4.1, in the case of θ_x approaching $\bar{\theta}_x^s$, the first passage time $E\{T_x\}$ approaches zero, nearly independently on the values σ_x takes. However, with increasing

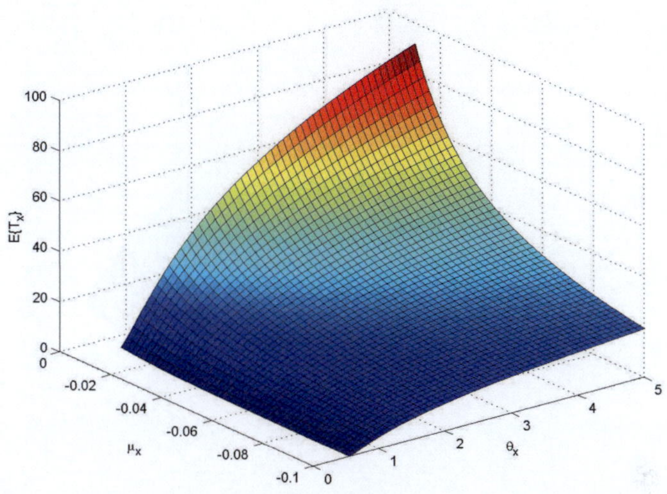

Figure 4.1: Expected first passage time $E\{T_x\}$ as a function of θ_x and μ_x

θ_x, the development of $E\{T_x\}$ resembles the positive branch of a root function. A smaller cash flow volatility expressed by smaller values of σ_x just lead to higher values of $E\{T_x\}$, while the shape of the curve stays the same.

Figure 4.3 pictures the influence of the salvage value SV in combination with the actual cash flow θ_x. The domains are $\theta_x \in [1.1214; 5]$ and $SV \in [0.05 \times SV, 2 \times SV] = [1, 20]$. As expected, small values of SV lead to high values of $E\{T_x\}$, whereas high values of SV lead to small values of $E\{T_x\}$. Additionally, figure 4.3 indicates that the influence of SV on the value maximizing bound $\bar{\theta}_x$ is higher in comparison to μ_x or σ_x.

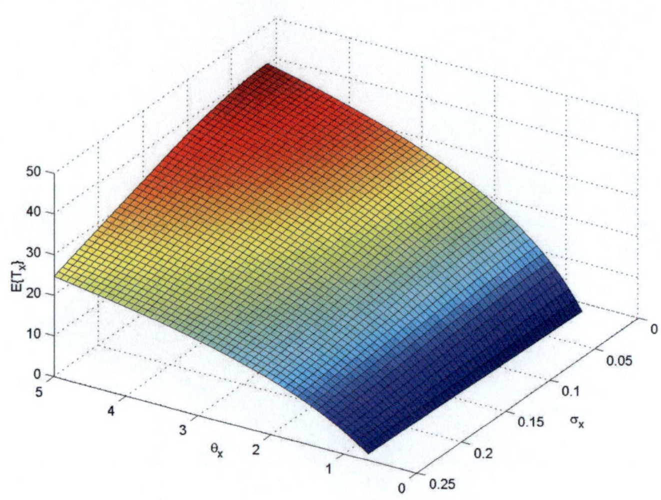

Figure 4.2: Expected first passage time $E\{T_x\}$ as a function of θ_x and σ_x

4.4.2.2 Effects of Market Factors on $E\{T_y\}$: Product Introduction

To investigate the influence of the parameters μ_y, σ_y, and SV on the expected first passage time $E\{T_y\}$, similar to section cf. 4.4.2.1, I generate 3-D figures comprising a variation of θ_y, and one further parameter, while the remaining stay constant.

The standard values of the following simulations are $r = 0.06$, $\mu_y = 0.05$, $\sigma_y = 0.25$, $\alpha = 0.9$, $c_y = 1$. The domain of one of these parameters is given by $\Phi_y \in [\Phi_y^b, \Phi_y^s]$; $\Phi_y = \mu_y, \sigma_y, SV$. Since I am interested in the combination of θ_y and Φ_y leading to $E\{T_y\} = 0$, the domain of θ_y determined by the starting point θ_{y0} and the bound $\bar{\theta}_y^s$ ($\theta_y \in [\theta_{y0}; \bar{\theta}_y^s]$). $\bar{\theta}_y^s$ is defined as $\bar{\theta}_y^s = \min\{\bar{\theta}_y(\Phi_y)\}$. Only the combinations of $\bar{\theta}_y^s$ and Φ_y^s will lead to

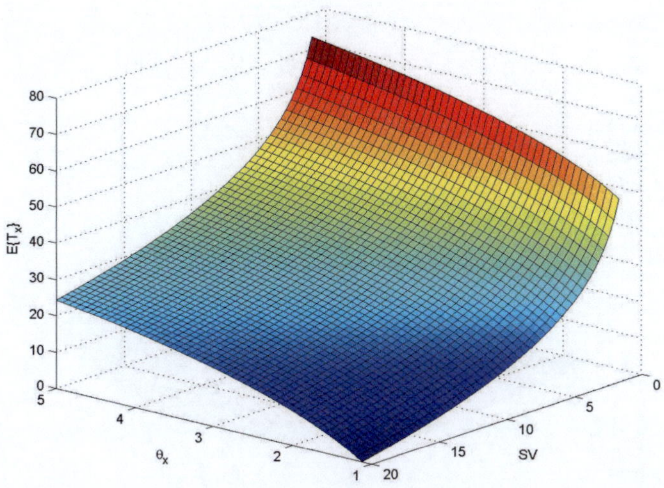

Figure 4.3: Expected first passage time $E\{T_x\}$ as a function of θ_x and SV

$E\{T_y\} = 0$. As far as $\bar{\theta}_y^s$ is a function of μ_y, σ_y, and SV, $\bar{\theta}_y^s$ must be anew calculated for each simulation.

Figure 4.4 shows the expected first passage time $E\{T_y\}$ as a function of the actual cash flow θ_y and the on average expected cash flow development μ_y. The domains are $\theta_y \in [1, 9.492]$ and $\mu_y \in [0.01, 0.05]$. The simulation results indicate that in the case of θ_y approaching the value maximizing bound $\bar{\theta}_y^s$, the expected cash flow development μ_y possesses only a small influence on $E\{T_y\}$. The influence of μ_y increases with smaller values of θ_y. Here, as expected, small values of μ_y extend the expected time of product introduction, whereas large values reduce $E\{T_y\}$.

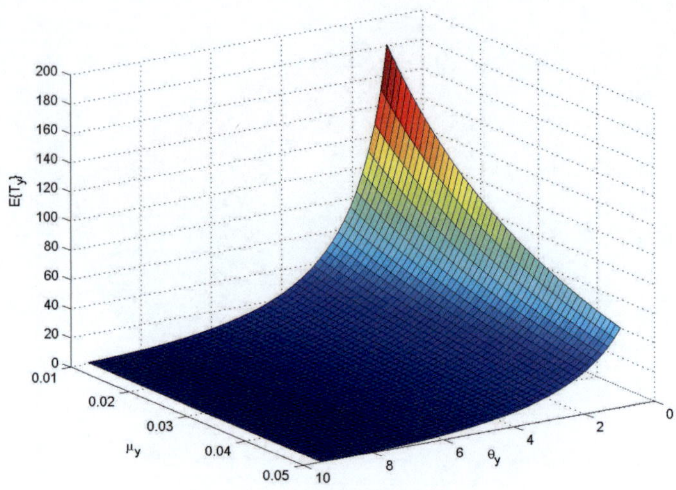

Figure 4.4: Expected first passage time $E\{T_y\}$ as a function of θ_y and μ_y

The next figure (figure 4.5), deals with the influence of the cash flow volatility σ_y of product y in combination with the actual cash flow θ_y, which the product y is able to generate on $E\{T_y\}$. The domains are given by $\theta_y \in [1, 6.0059]$ and $\sigma_y \in [0.01, 0.5]$. The expected first time passage $E\{T_y\}$ is equal to 0 by θ_y reaching the trigger bound $\bar{\theta}_y^s$ in combination with a cash flow volatility of approximately 1 %. Increasing values of σ_y lead to higher values of the optimal trigger bound $\bar{\theta}_y$ with the consequence that values of $E\{T_y\}$ increase. However, the influence of σ_y on $E\{T_y\}$ is small in comparison to θ_y values detaching from $\bar{\theta}_y$. In other words, and decrease of θ_y leads to an exponential increase of $E\{T_y\}$. Consequently, the highest values of $E\{T_y\}$ arise on account of a combination of high values of σ_y and small values of θ_y.

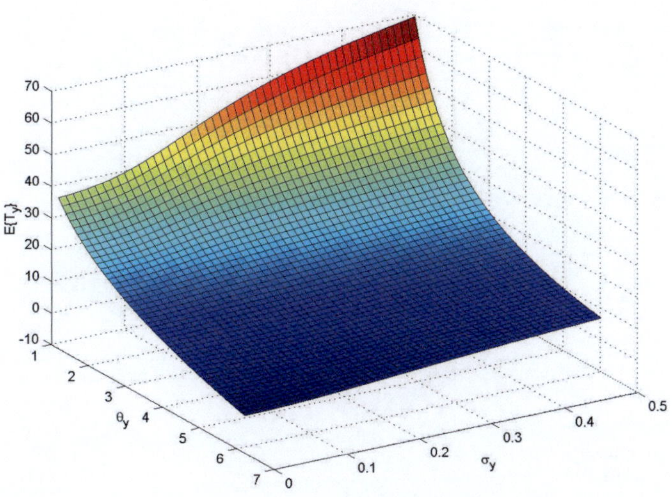

Figure 4.5: Expected first passage time $E\{T_y\}$ as a function of θ_y and σ_y

By means of figure 4.6, I examine the influence of the investment costs IC in combination with the actual cash flow generation θ_y with the expected time to introduce product y to the market. Using an approach analogous to the previous simulations, the domains are given by $\theta_y \in [1, 4.7465]$ and $IC \in [0.5 \times IC, 2 \times IC] = [50, 200]$. In the case of θ_y reaching $\bar{\theta}_y^s$, the expected first passage time $E\{T_y\}$ is equal to 0. Even if θ_y drifts from the value maximizing bound $\bar{\theta}_y^s$ (e.g. $3 \leq \theta_y \leq \bar{\theta}_y^s$), I recognize that small investment costs (in this case $IC \approx 50$) press down the expected first passage time $E\{T_y\}$ toward 0. However, a further deviation of θ_y from $\bar{\theta}_y^s$ (e.g. $\theta_y \leq 3$) leads to an exponential increase of $E\{T_y\}$.

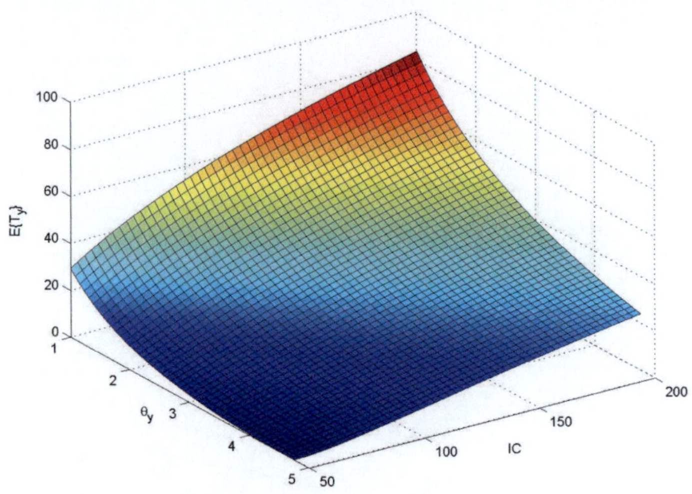

Figure 4.6: Expected first passage time $E\{T_y\}$ as a function of θ_y and IC

On the other hand, under the condition of $\theta_y \approx \bar{\theta}_y^s$, increasing investment costs lead to higher values of $\bar{\theta}_y$ which results in an approximately linear increase of $E\{T_y\}$.

As expected, the highest values of $E\{T_y\}$ are based on a combination of small assumed cash flows generated by product y and high investment costs to produce and introduce the product to the market.

4.5 Discussions, Limitations & Future Research of the Third Research Objective

To ensure long-term success of companies operating in fast changing markets it is essential to achieve product and process improvements, and, at the same time to follow, respectively to induce, disruptive product and process innovations in emerging markets.

In the literature of this field the first aim is described as exploitation (March 1991). It incorporates characteristics such as efficiency, control, variance reduction, and short-term profits (O'Reilly & Tushman 2007). The second aim is described as exploration (March 1991). Exploration is aligned with attributes such as search, innovation, variation, and future profits (O'Reilly & Tushman 2007). The concept of ambidexterity deals with the requirements firms must fulfill to support both approaches simultaneously (Duncan 1976).

In a variety of research contributions concerning organizational design (Tushman & O'Reilly 1996, Adler et al. 1999, Gibson & Birkinshaw 2004, Jansen et al. 2005), strategy (Burgelman 1991, Burgelman 2002, O'Reilly & Tushman 2007), organizational learning (Vassolo, Anand & Folta 2004, Vermeulen & Barkema 2001, Benner & Tushman 2003, He & Wong 2004, Gupta et al. 2006), and technological innovation (Atuahene-Gima 2005, Benner & Tushman 2003, Danneels 2002, Smith & Tushman 2005) researchers discuss how to integrate explorative and exploitative activities in order to form successful ambidextrous organizations (Raisch & Birkinshaw 2008).

In this context researchers recognize the importance and difficulty of balancing these obviously diametrical requirements to enable exploitation and exploration simultaneously (Adler et al. 1999, Brown & Duguid 2001, Katila & Ahuja 2002). March (1991, p. 105) states that "the basic problem confronting an organization is to engage in sufficient exploitation to ensure its current viability and, at the same time, devote enough energy to exploration to ensure its future viability". Because of the pressure to satisfy current customer needs and short-term profits researchers assume that firms often tend to push exploitation while neglecting exploration (Henderson & Clark 1990, Levinthal & March 1993, Gupta et al. 2006).

Even though researchers are aware of the firms' challenge to find an optimal balance of explorative and exploitative activities, until now an appropriate instruments is still missing that supports firms to identify the optimal balance of exploration and exploitation. In this research contribution I have developed such an instrument based on real options insights.

For this purpose, I assume that the optimal balance of exploration and exploitation depends largely on environmental changes (Tushman & Romanelli 1985, Tushman & O'Reilly 1996, Volberda 1996, Feldman & Pentland 2003, Probst & Raisch 2005). In particular, I assume that substantial environmental shifts with regard to ambidextrous organizations are declining and emerging markets. In declining markets firms attempt to extend the profitable sale of products by exploitative activities such as continuous and incremental technological improvements, quality increase and cost reductions. Emerging markets incorporate opportunities and threats at the same time. Threats, since emerging markets present platforms to attack incumbents in other markets, opportunities, since explorative activities may generate products which are superior to those of competitors.

The firms are now challenged to understand how long an engagement in a declining market is most profitable or, in other words how long exploitative activities should last. At the same time firms have to understand when it is most profitable to enter an emerging market in order to allocate resources in advance towards explorative activities.

Following this line of reasoning the near at hand target dimension to infer an optimal ratio of exploitation and exploration is the firm's cumulative, expected profit with regard to declining and emerging markets.

Based on these insights and assumptions I have outlined a mathematical model presenting one firm selling a product in a declining market, and having the option to enter an emerging market. With regard to my model, the basic insight is that there exist profit maximizing points in time when to discard a product from a declining market and when to launch a product into an emerging market (Theorem 1). Discarding a product from a declining market means to taper off and finally to terminate exploitative activities. Preparing the entry and entering an emerging market means to stress explorative activities, which are terminated respectively transformed into exploitative activities when the market entry is performed. The sources of both kinds of activities are underlying resources.

Due to my model assumptions the profit maximizing point in time can only be determined in real-time. Since resource allocations cannot take place in time infinitely short, but must be planned, prepared and executed in advance to avoid resource conflicts, it is of crucial interest to firm's decision makers to predict the cash flow maximizing point in time with regard to a product introduction or withdrawal. However, I am able to predict the length of time until the expected profit maximizing point in time is reached (Theorem 2). Since the model incorporates the factors that determine this duration, I am also able to analyze the impact of the different influence factors on the expected profit maximizing point in time.

The results of my model have an impact on current ambidextrous research. They support researchers to better understand and to resolve a fundamental problem, precisely to identify the optimal balance of exploitation and exploration (March 1991). Using the expected profit as a target dimension, I am able to demonstrate that an optimal balance of exploration and exploitation can be inferred.

Furthermore, based on my model I am able to confirm the assumption that explorative and exploitative activities depend largely on external factors (Gibson & Birkinshaw 2004, Levinthal & March 1993, Siggelkow & Levinthal 2003, Jansen et al. 2005). Yet, they reveal further influence factors such as the growth rates of markets, the market volatility, the investment costs to enter an emerging market and the salvage that value firms obtain when discarding a declining market. Here, I have generated 3-D plots to clarify in a first step the influence of these factors on the expected time to terminate exploitative or explorative activities. To gain a better understanding of the impact of these factors on the profit maximizing point in time, a generalized investigation of the underlying equations or simulations considering the ration of different influence factors could be promising future research objectives.

Besides academic insights my model provides a plurality of normative implications. For instance, the results of my basic model are sufficient to show that by the application of an appropriate model, firms' decision makers are able to predict and specify the profit maximizing point in time to discard products from declining markets and to launch products into emerging markets. Based on this knowledge managers are able to taper off and then terminate exploitative activities or to stress explorative activities till they should be transformed into exploitative activities. This capacity enables firms' decision makers to avoid resource conflicts and to accomplish a most efficient allocation of resources. In short, it supports managers to overcome a basic problem of ambidextrous organizations, namely to balance exploitation and exploration in an optimal way (March 1991) along the time-line with regard to environmental shifts.

Such a model is also useful to support firms' decision makers to formulate a compelling strategy that emphasizes the importance of being simultaneously committed to both, exploitation and exploration activities (O'Reilly & Tushman 2007). Since firms tend towards exploitation (Henderson & Clark 1990, Levinthal & March 1993, Gupta et al. 2006) this model may also strengthen long-term thinking of top management, and employees as a prerequisite for a sustainable implementation of ambidexterity (Devan, Millan & Shirke 2005).

The primary aim of my research contribution is to provide a solution of one of the most challenging problems in ambidextrous research, that is to overcome the difficulty of balancing exploitation and exploration in a sustaining way. To accomplish this research object, I outlined a simple model consisting of one firm selling a product in a declining market and having the option to enter an emerging market. However, due to this simplicity, the model suffers most likely the limitation of not being applicable in reality. Consequently, a future research avenue is, in particular with regard to the normative capacity of this model, to identify a firm as a cooperation partner facing the problem to balance exploitative and explorative activities. A model outlined to support this firm to optimally balance exploration and exploitation along the time line will most likely lead to a broader understanding of ambidextrous organizations.

Chapter 5

Summary

In my dissertation I pursue three research objectives. The central aim of the first research objective has been to discuss if and how an industry independent investigation of dynamic capabilities is possible (chapter 2). The second research objective comprises an analysis of the value implications of dynamic capabilities (chapter 3). The third research objective deals with the optimal balance of exploitative and explorative activities depending on market changes (chapter 4). To ensure a smooth transition towards the main part of each chapter, I start each chapter with a "tailer-made" introduction, embedding my research objective in the decisive literature and provide an extensive description of each research objective. I also describe my approach to the investigation of the research objectives and anticipate the results including the normative and academic implications. In the main parts of each chapter I pursue the research objectives. I conclude each chapter with a discussion of my research, place the results in the context of the relevant literature, emphasize the academic and normative implications of my research, and show its limitations but also its future avenues. This chapter serves to conclude my dissertation. To avoid redundance and repetition with regard the introduction and conclusion of each chapter, in the following I focus on summarizing the basic notion of each research objective as well as on their normative and academic impacts.

Researchers emphasize the strategic importance of capabilities, since a plurality of different factors make these complex, interwoven routines work, and, therefore, are hard to imitate (Teece et al. 1997). However, the effectiveness and efficiency of capabilities may decrease in comparison to those of competitors because of environmental shifts over time (Lavie 2006). To maintain competitive advantage, firms' inherent institutions, generally described as dynamic capabilities, are essential to adapt capabilities to actual or conceivable conditions (Zott 2003, Lavie 2006, Schreyögg & Kliesch-Eberl 2007).

On account of the obvious strategic importance to firms to achieve and maintain competitive advantage in the long run, this new research area has grown especially during the last 20 years. Some of this literature focuses on the description, the definition, and the functionality, as well as on the antecedents and consequences of dynamic capabilities (Teece et al. 1997, Helfat & Raubitschek 2000, Makadok 2001, Zollo & Winter 2002, Benner & Tushman 2003, Helfat & Peteraf 2003, Winter 2003, Lavie 2006, Schreyögg & Kliesch-Eberl 2007).

Reviewing dynamic capability literature I have identified three research objectives. The first research objective deals with the fact that despite the plurality of research contributions there neither exists an empirical investigation of dynamic capabilities across industries, nor a dynamic capability concept that supports such a challenge. Accordingly, the primary aim of my first research contribution is to discuss if an empirical investigation across industries is feasible, and then to identify the characteristics of such a model.

To accomplish this research objective I follow Webster & Watson's (2002) approach, first to perform a literature review and then to propose a concept based on the gained insights. In this context, I notice that researchers postulate that effectiveness is based on the application of stable patterns (Zahra et al. 2006, Helfat et al. 2007), and, therefore, conclude that the functions establishing dynamic capabilities must be structured in a particular, but industry boarder crossing way (Eisenhardt & Martin (2000) → equifinality of dynamic capabilities, cf. section 2.2.3). Consequently the best way to present reality seems to be an approach appropriate to describe dynamic capabilities as a complex unity consisting of different, interwoven elements, which are firm specific in their occurrence, scope and interplay, but at the same time are based on specific functional principles. This reasoning explains the possibility to develop an across industries applicable instrument to prove the existence, functionality and effectiveness of dynamic capabilities. Consequently, I outline a first approach to analyze dynamic capabilities in an industry-crossing way.

In recent literature, researchers have undertaken similar efforts to outline models appropriate to operationalize dynamic capabilities (Wang & Ahmed 2007, Ambrosini & Bowman 2009, Barreto 2010). Even though various approaches to develop these models are similar, the models themselves differ largely in their central aspects. Accordingly, a plurality of oppositional points and critical issues arise. However, since the dynamic capabilities concept is most promising to reveal the long-term success of firms, the next step in this research should be a further discussion and then to drive forward a dynamic capability concept suitable to execute empirical investigations of dynamic capabilities across industries. Apart from the academic implications to deepen and validate the understanding of how dynamic capabilities ensure long-term competitive advantage of firms, this research objective also has normative implications. Taking my concept or similar concepts as a basis researchers should be able to infer rules or principles of how firms' decision makers should behave to maintain success of firms in changing and uncertain environments.

A further central issue of dynamic capability research is to understand the interrelationship between dynamic capabilities, the value generating resource base and firm performance. Here, a number of researchers assume that dynamic capabilities influence firm performance indirectly via the appropriate adaptation of the resource bases with regard to environmental shifts (Teece et al. 1997, Eisenhardt & Martin 2000, Zott 2003, Lavie 2006, Zahra et al. 2006).

To deepen this research issue I change the perspective and considere the possibility that dynamic capabilities possess value similar to the value generating resource base, even in a "dormant" state. This approach leads to further research questions, in particular the questions of how dynamic capabilities influence firm value and furthermore which factors influence the value of dynamic capabilities.

Summarized, my second research objective deals with the investigation of the value implications of dynamic capabilities. Based on insights of Kogut & Kulatilaka (2001) and Kyläheiko et al. (2002) I apply real option knowledge to approach this research objective. The results of my model leads to the insight that the value of a firm is composed of the expected, discounted values, generated by the firm's resource base, *and* the values of its dynamic capabilities to modify the firm's resource base. My model enables me to identify the value driving factors of dynamic capabilities. Using 3-D plots I investigate exemplarily their influence on the value of dynamic capabilities. Furthermore, I demonstrate the effects of an inappropriate application of dynamic capabilities in terms of time and even in case of the absence of dynamic capabilities.

These results do not only deepen the understanding or even open new ways to consider dynamic capabilities, but they also possess normative implications. Assuming for instance that firms are value maximizers the value of dynamic capabilities is given by external factors. The only factor that firms can use to influence the value of dynamic capabilities, and thus the firm value, is the application of dynamic capabilities in terms of time. Accordingly, the results of my model emphasize the importance of applying dynamic capabilities at a specific point in time (Teece 2007) in order to maximize firm value, and, at the same time, they confute the assumption that the competitive advantage of firms results from applying dynamic capabilities sooner in comparison to competitors (Eisenhardt & Martin 2000). In other words, ceteris paribus, the astute use of dynamic capabilities in terms of times seems to be decisive (Eisenhardt & Martin 2000).

My third research objective is designed to provide answer to a problem scholars assume to be central in ambidextrous research, namely to find the optimal balance of explorative and exploitative activities (March 1991). Simplified, exploitation means to ensure the "earning now" via efficiency, increasing productivity, control, certainty, and variance reduction (O'Reilly & Tushman 2007), while exploitation means to prepare or be prepared for future or emerging markets via search, discovery, autonomy, innovation and embracing variation (O'Reilly & Tushman 2007). The balance of both, exploration and exploitation depends on the resources a firm provides to support these activities. Assuming changing environments, a progressional adaptation of the ratio of exploration to exploitation implying an appropriate resource base adaptation is essential to ensure the current and long term competitive advantage. Therefore, even though my third research objective is outlined to pursue a specific issue of ambidextrous research, it is, because of the underlying resource base adaptation, part of dynamic capability research.

Despite a general awareness of the importance to find the optimal ratio of exploitation to exploration, in ambidexterity research, there exist no instruments, neither to determine nor to predict the optimal point in time to withdraw a product from a declining market in order to taper off and then to stop exploitative activities, or to enter an emerging market by launching a new product in order to stress explorative activities in advance and then to transform these activities into exploitative activities.

Using real options knowledge I am able to outline a formal model based on the assumption that a firm makes efforts to exploit a declining market and at the same time stresses explorative activities to be prepared to enter an emerging market.

Using profit maximization as the target dimension I am able to determine and predict the optimal points in time to withdraw a product from a declining market and to launch a product into an emerging market. Based on this information an optimal balance of explorative and exploitative activities including the necessary resource based adaptation can be inferred.

Apart from the academic implications of my research contributions to provide answers to a fundamental issue in ambidextrous research (March 1991), the outline and the results of my model have normative implications. An adapted model should support managers to optimize the balance of a firm's exploitative and explorative activities.

Appendix A

Calculation of the Maximal Firm Value

A.1 Derivation of the PDE I

I assume that the value generations of the capabilities x and y follow a geometric Brown'ian Motion with the expectation value μ, the variance σ^2, and the noise described by a Wiener process $(W(t) \sim N(0, t))$:

$$d\theta_x(t) = \mu_x \theta_x(t) dt + \sigma_x \theta_x(t) dW_x(t) \qquad \text{(A.1)}$$

$$d\theta_y(t) = \mu_y \theta_y(t) dt + \sigma_y \theta_y(t) dW_y(t). \qquad \text{(A.2)}$$

I further assume $\mu_x < 0$, $0 < \mu_y < r$ and $dW_x(t) \neq dW_y(t)$, $E(dW_x dW_y) = 0$ and use the notation of θ_x respectively θ_y for $\theta_x(t)$ respectively $\theta_y(t)$, etc..

The firm strives to maximize the over time accumulated cash flow and faces the decision problem described by equation A.3

$$
\begin{aligned}
V_{Max}(\theta_x, \theta_y) \;=\;& \max_{\tau_1, \tau_2} E \left\{ \int_0^{\tau_1} \left[\alpha\theta_x(t) + c_0(1-\alpha)\theta_y(t) \right] e^{-rt} dt + SV e^{-\tau_1} \right. \\
&+ \left. \int_{\tau_1}^{\tau_2} c_0\theta_y(t) e^{-r(t-\tau_2)} dt - qICe^{-\tau_2} + \int_{\tau_2}^{\infty} qc_0\theta_y e^{-r(t-\tau_2)} dt \right\}.
\end{aligned} \tag{A.3}
$$

The continuation value of equation A.3 is given by:

$$
rV(\theta_x, \theta_y)dt = [\alpha\theta_x + c_0(1-\alpha)\theta_y]dt + E(dV). \tag{A.4}
$$

Because $V(\theta_x, \theta_y)$ is a function dependent on two diffusion processes, I use Itô's "two-dimensional" Lemma to specify dV of equation A.4:

$$
\begin{aligned}
dV \;=\;& \frac{\partial V}{\partial \theta_x} d\theta_x + \frac{\partial V}{\partial \theta_y} d\theta_y \\
&+ \frac{1}{2} \frac{\partial^2 V}{\partial \theta_x^2} (d\theta_x)^2 + \frac{1}{2} \frac{\partial^2 V}{\partial \theta_y^2} (d\theta_y)^2 \\
&+ \frac{\partial^2 V}{\partial \theta_x \partial \theta_y} d\theta_x d\theta_y.
\end{aligned} \tag{A.5}
$$

In general, $d\theta_x d\theta_y$ can be expressed by equation A.6

$$
d\theta_x d\theta_y = \rho\sigma_x\theta_x\sigma_y\theta_y dt. \tag{A.6}
$$

The independency of $d\theta_x$ and $d\theta_y$ ($E(dW_x dW_y = 0)$) is expressed by $\rho = 0$. Therefore, I obtain:

$$
d\theta_x d\theta_y = \rho\sigma_x\theta_x\sigma_y\theta_y dt = 0. \tag{A.7}
$$

Furthermore, neglecting terms with an order of $dt > 1$ ($\Rightarrow (d\theta_x)^2 = \sigma_x^2\theta_x^2 dt$, $(d\theta_y)^2 = \sigma_y^2\theta_y^2 dt$), A.5 can be simplified to equation A.8:

$$
\begin{aligned}
dV \;=\;& \frac{\partial V}{\partial \theta_x}d\theta_x + \frac{\partial V}{\partial \theta_y}d\theta_y \\[2mm]
+\;& \frac{1}{2}\sigma_x^2\theta_x^2\frac{\partial^2 V}{\partial \theta_x^2}dt + \frac{1}{2}\sigma_y^2\theta_y^2\frac{\partial^2 V}{\partial \theta_y^2}dt.
\end{aligned}
\tag{A.8}
$$

Hence, the expectation value $E\{dV\}$ is:

$$
\begin{aligned}
E\{dV\} \;=\;& E\left\{\frac{\partial V}{\partial \theta_x}[\mu_x\theta_x dt + \sigma_x\theta_x dW_x]\right\} \\[2mm]
+\;& E\left\{\frac{\partial V}{\partial \theta_y}[\mu_y\theta_y dt + \sigma_y\theta_y dW_y]\right\} \\[2mm]
+\;& E\left\{\frac{1}{2}\sigma_x^2\theta_x^2\frac{\partial^2 V}{\partial \theta_x^2}dt + \frac{1}{2}\sigma_y^2\theta_y^2\frac{\partial^2 V}{\partial \theta_y^2}dt\right\} \\[2mm]
+\;& E\left\{\sigma_x\sigma_y\theta_x\theta_y\frac{\partial^2 V}{\partial \theta_x\partial \theta_y}dt\right\} \\[2mm]
=\;& \mu_x\theta_x\frac{\partial V}{\partial \theta_x}dt + \mu_y\theta_y\frac{\partial V}{\partial \theta_y}dt + \frac{1}{2}\sigma_x^2\theta_x^2\frac{\partial^2 V}{\partial \theta_x^2}dt \\[2mm]
+\;& \frac{1}{2}\sigma_y^2\theta_y^2\frac{\partial^2 V}{\partial \theta_y^2}dt,
\end{aligned}
\tag{A.9}
$$

which leads me to the following partial differential equation:

$$
\begin{aligned}
0 \;=\;& -rV + \alpha\theta_x + c_0(1-\alpha)\theta_y + \mu_x\theta_x\frac{\partial V}{\partial \theta_x} + \mu_y\theta_y\frac{\partial V}{\partial \theta_y} \\[2mm]
+\;& \frac{1}{2}\sigma_x^2\theta_x^2\frac{\partial^2 V}{\partial \theta_x^2} + \frac{1}{2}\sigma_y^2\theta_y^2\frac{\partial^2 V}{\partial \theta_y^2}.
\end{aligned}
\tag{A.10}
$$

The overall solution of this partial differential equation consists of a particulate solution and of a general solution of the homogeneous part of the differential equation.

A.2   Particulate Solution of the PDE I

Assuming $V_p(\theta_x, \theta_y) = a\theta_x + b\theta_y$ delivers with $a = \frac{\alpha}{r-\mu_x}$ and $b = \frac{c_0(1-\alpha)}{r-\mu_y}$ a possible solution:

$$V_p(\theta_x, \theta_y) = \frac{\alpha}{r - \mu_x}\theta_x + \frac{c_0(1 - \alpha)}{r - \mu_y}\theta_y. \tag{A.11}$$

A.3   General Solution of the Homogeneous Part of the PDE I

The homogeneous part of the differential equation is expressed by:

$$
\begin{aligned}
0 \;=\;& \mu_x\theta_x\frac{\partial V}{\partial\theta_x} + \mu_y\theta_y\frac{\partial V}{\partial\theta_y} \\
+\;& \frac{1}{2}\sigma_x^2\theta_x^2\frac{\partial^2 V}{\partial\theta_x^2} + \frac{1}{2}\sigma_y^2\theta_y^2\frac{\partial^2 V}{\partial\theta_y^2} \\
-\,& rV.
\end{aligned}
\tag{A.12}
$$

A possible solution may deliver the following approach:

$$V_h(\theta_x, \theta_y) = A\theta_x^\gamma + B\theta_y^\varepsilon. \tag{A.13}$$

Introducing the guess $V_h(\theta_x, \theta_y)$ and the required derivations lead me to equation A.14

$$
\begin{aligned}
0 \;=\;& -rA\theta_x^\gamma - rB\theta_y^\varepsilon + A\gamma\mu_x\theta_x^\gamma + B\varepsilon\mu_y\theta_y^\varepsilon \\
+\;& \frac{1}{2}\gamma(\gamma - 1)A\sigma_x^2\theta_x^\gamma + \frac{1}{2}\varepsilon(\varepsilon - 1)B\sigma_y^2\theta_y^\varepsilon \\
=\;& A\theta_x^\gamma\left[-r + \gamma\mu_x + \frac{1}{2}\gamma(\gamma - 1)\sigma_x^2\right] \\
+\;& B\theta_y^\varepsilon\left[-r + \varepsilon\mu_y + \frac{1}{2}\varepsilon(\varepsilon - 1)\sigma_y^2\right].
\end{aligned}
\tag{A.14}
$$

This equation is fulfilled by

$$\gamma_{1,2} = \frac{1}{2} - \frac{\mu_x}{\sigma_x^2} \pm \sqrt{\left(\frac{1}{2} - \frac{\mu_x}{\sigma_x^2}\right)^2 + \frac{2r}{\sigma_x^2}} \tag{A.15}$$

and

$$\varepsilon_{1,2} = \frac{1}{2} - \frac{\mu_y}{\sigma_y^2} \pm \sqrt{\left(\frac{1}{2} - \frac{\mu_y}{\sigma_y^2}\right)^2 + \frac{2r}{\sigma_y^2}}. \tag{A.16}$$

Hence, the solution of the differential equation is:

$$
\begin{aligned}
V(\theta_x, \theta_y) \;&=\; V_p + V_h \tag{A.17}\\[6pt]
&=\; a\theta_x + A_1\theta_x^{\gamma_1} + A_2\theta_x^{\gamma_2}\\[6pt]
&+\; b\theta_y + B_1\theta_y^{\varepsilon_1} + B_2\theta_y^{\varepsilon_2}\\[6pt]
&=\; \frac{\alpha}{r - \mu_x}\theta_x + A_1\theta_x^{\gamma_1} + A_2\theta_x^{\gamma_2}\\[6pt]
&+\; \frac{c_0(1 - \alpha)}{r - \mu_y}\theta_y + B_1\theta_y^{\varepsilon_1} + B_2\theta_y^{\varepsilon_2}.
\end{aligned}
$$

The terms $\frac{\alpha}{r-\mu_x}\theta_x$ and $\frac{c_0(1-\alpha)}{r-\mu_y}\theta_y$ describe the value generation of the applied capabilities x and y. The factors $A_1\theta_x^{\gamma_1}$ and $A_2\theta_x^{\gamma_2}$ describe the option value to abandon capability x, and $B_1\theta_y^{\varepsilon_1}$ and $B_2\theta_y^{\varepsilon_2}$ to extend capability y from the scope c_0 to qc_0. The optimal value to abandon capability x and to shift the amount α of vacant resources used to execute capability x to support capability y is given by $\bar{\theta}_x$. The optimal value to enlarge the scope of resources to apply capability y from c_0 to qc_0 is given by $\bar{\theta}_y$. To determine the values of A_1, A_2, B_1 and B_2 as well as the bounds $\bar{\theta}_{x,y}$ by using the value matching and smooth pasting conditions, I have to describe the next production step.

A.4   Derivation of the PDE II

Here, I assume that the firm abandons the capability x to the advantage of capability y before the enlargement of capability y took place. Therefore, the firm strives to maximize the over time accumulated cash ow and, now, faces the decision problem described by equation A.18:

$$V(\theta_y)_{MAX} = E\left\{\int_{\tau_1}^{\tau_2} c_0\theta_y e^{-r(t-\tau_1)}dt + \int_{\tau_2}^{\infty} qc_0\theta_y e^{-r(t-\tau_2)}dt\right\}. \tag{A.18}$$

An equivalent description is given by equation A.19

$$rVdt = c_0\theta_y dt + E(dV). \tag{A.19}$$

Using Itô's lemma dV is expressed by A.20:

$$dV = \frac{\partial V}{\partial \theta_y}d\theta_y + \frac{1}{2}\frac{\partial^2 V}{\partial \theta_y^2}(d\theta_y)^2. \tag{A.20}$$

I obtain the differential equation A.21 by inserting the expectation value of dV in equation A.19:

$$0 = \theta_y + \mu_y\theta_y\frac{\partial V}{\partial \theta_y} + \frac{1}{2}\sigma_y^2\theta_y^2\frac{\partial^2 V}{\partial \theta_y^2} - rV. \tag{A.21}$$

A.5   Solution of the PDE II

The approach $V = \theta_y^\lambda$ leads to the characteristic equation:

$$\lambda^2 + \left(\frac{2\mu_y}{\sigma_y^2} - 1\right)\lambda - \frac{2r}{\sigma_y^2} = 0. \tag{A.22}$$

Hence, $\lambda_{1,2}$ are:

$$\lambda_{1,2} = \frac{1}{2} - \frac{\mu_y}{\sigma_y^2} \pm \sqrt{\left(\frac{1}{2} - \frac{\mu_y}{\sigma_y^2}\right)^2 + \frac{2r}{\sigma_y^2}}. \tag{A.23}$$

Because the perturbation factor θ_y follows the form θ_y^{α} I use the approach $C(\ln\theta_y)^k\theta_y^{\alpha}$ with $k = 0$ ($\alpha \neq \lambda_{1,2}$) and $\alpha = 1$. Using this approach in equation B.21 results in

$$C = \frac{c_0}{r - \mu_y}. \tag{A.24}$$

Hence, the solution of the differential equation B.16 is:

$$V(\theta_y) = \frac{c_0}{r - \mu_y}\theta_y + C_1\theta_y^{\lambda_1} + C_2\theta_y^{\lambda_2}. \tag{A.25}$$

$\frac{c_0}{r-\mu_y}\theta_y$ represents the generated value by the capability y. $C_1\theta_y^{\lambda_1}$ and $C_2\theta_y^{\lambda_2}$ are used to determine the value of future options.

A.6 Determination of Coefficients

To determine the coefficients $A_{1,2}$, $B_{1,2}$ and $C_{1,2}$ and the optimal value of $\bar{\theta}_x$ at which dynamic capabilities should be applied to execute the change of the resource base I use the value matching and smooth pasting condition:

$$\begin{aligned} VM_x(\bar{\theta}_x, \theta_y) &= SV + \frac{c_0}{r - \mu_y}\theta_y + C_1\theta_y^{\lambda_1} + C_2\theta_y^{\lambda_2} \tag{A.26}\\ &= A_1\bar{\theta}_x^{\gamma_1} + A_2\bar{\theta}_x^{\gamma_2} + B_1\theta_y^{\varepsilon_1} + B_2\theta_y^{\varepsilon_2} + \frac{\alpha}{r - \mu_x}\bar{\theta}_x + \frac{c_0(1 - \alpha)}{r - \mu_y}\theta_y. \end{aligned}$$

In consideration of the co-domains of $\gamma_{1,2}$ ($\gamma_1 > 1 \wedge \gamma_2 < 0$) the use of the solution γ_1 would lead to a negative option value which has no economic implication (no bubble condition).

Additionally, as far as equation A.26 must be fulfilled for all $\theta_y \in \mathbf{R}^{\geq 0}$, I set $\theta_y = 0$.

The value matching condition simplifies to:

$$VM_x(\bar{\theta}_x) = SV = A_2\bar{\theta}_x^{\gamma_2} + \frac{\alpha}{r - \mu_x}\bar{\theta}_x. \tag{A.27}$$

Accordingly, the value matching condition of capability x is given by equation A.28:

$$SP_x(\bar{\theta}_x) = 0 = \frac{\alpha}{r - \mu_x} + A_2\gamma_2\bar{\theta}_x^{\gamma_2-1}. \tag{A.28}$$

Using equation A.27 and A.28 I obtain:

$$A_2 = \frac{\alpha\bar{\theta}_x}{\gamma_2(\mu_x - r)}\bar{\theta}_x^{-\gamma_2} = A, \tag{A.29}$$

and

$$\bar{\theta}_x = \frac{r - \mu_x}{\alpha}\;\frac{\gamma_2}{\gamma_2 - 1}SV. \tag{A.30}$$

However, it is important to notice that the determination of A and $\bar{\theta}_x$ is independent of the value development of θ_y. Therefore, it is not necessary to do any examinations concerning $\bar{\theta}_x$ because of other constellations of y.

Next, I consider the extension of capability y from scope c_0 to qc_0 at a point in time at which capability x has already been given up in advantage to capability y. The description of this situation has already been presented through the equations A.18 and A.19. Because of the co-domains of $\varepsilon_{1,2}$ ($\varepsilon_1 > 1 \wedge \varepsilon_2 < 0$) B_2 does not provide a positive option value. Consequently, the value matching condition is given by equation A.31 and the value matching condition by equation A.32

$$VM_y(\bar{\theta}_y) = \frac{qc_0}{r - \mu_y}\bar{\theta}_y - qIC = B_1\bar{\theta}_y^{\varepsilon_1} + \frac{c_0}{r - \mu_y}\bar{\theta}_y \tag{A.31}$$

$$SP_y(\bar{\theta}_y) = \frac{qc_0}{r - \mu_y} = \frac{c_0}{r - \mu_y} + B_1\varepsilon_1\bar{\theta}_y^{\varepsilon_1-1}. \tag{A.32}$$

Equations A.31 and A.32 enable me to determine B_1 and $\bar{\theta}_{yp}$:

$$\bar{\theta}_{yp} = \frac{\varepsilon_1}{\varepsilon_1 - 1} \frac{r - \mu_y}{c_0(q - 1)}qIC. \tag{A.33}$$

$$B_1 = \frac{c_0(q - 1)\bar{\theta}_y}{\varepsilon_1(r - \mu_y)}\bar{\theta}_y^{-\varepsilon_1} = B \tag{A.34}$$

However, contrary to the calculations of $\bar{\theta}_x$, changes concerning the capability x affect the value of $\bar{\theta}_y$. As I have already determined $\bar{\theta}_{yp}$ from the starting point that the resources of capability x are already used to support capability y I determine $\bar{\theta}_{ya}$ under the assumption that the capability x has not yet been handed over. The starting point of these calculations is given by the equations A.35 and A.36:

$$V(\theta_x, \theta_y) \equiv E\left\{\int_{\tau_1}^{\tau_2} c_0(1 - \alpha)\theta_y e^{-r(t-\tau_1)}dt + \int_{\tau_2}^{\infty} qc_0(1 - \alpha)\theta_y e^{-r(t-\tau_2)}dt\right\}. \tag{A.35}$$

$$rVdt = c_0(1 - \alpha)\theta_y dt + E(dV). \tag{A.36}$$

The calculation based on this starting point leads to $\bar{\theta}_{ya}$ based on the investment $q(1 - \alpha)IC$, since I assume that the investment costs are proportionally depending on the capability extension:

$$\bar{\theta}_{ya} = \frac{\varepsilon}{\varepsilon - 1} \frac{r - \mu_y}{c_0(q - 1)} \frac{q(1 - \alpha)IC}{(1 - \alpha)} = \frac{\varepsilon}{\varepsilon - 1} \frac{r - \mu_y}{c_0(q - 1)}qIC = \bar{\theta}_{yp} = \bar{\theta}_y \tag{A.37}$$

To summarize, the calculation of $V(\theta_x, \theta_y)$ depends on the values of θ_x and θ_y:

$$V(\theta_x, \theta_y) = \begin{cases} \frac{\alpha}{r-\mu_x}\theta_x + \frac{(1-\alpha)c_0}{r-\mu_y}\theta_y + A\theta_x^{\gamma_2} + B\theta_y^{\varepsilon_1} & : & \theta_x > \bar{\theta}_x \wedge \theta_y < \bar{\theta}_y \\[2ex] \frac{c_0}{r-\mu_y}\theta_y + B\theta_y^{\varepsilon_1} & : & \theta_x < \bar{\theta}_x \wedge \theta_y < \bar{\theta}_y \\[2ex] \frac{qc_0}{r-\mu_y}\theta_y & : & \theta_x < \bar{\theta}_x \wedge \theta_y > \bar{\theta}_y \\[2ex] \frac{\alpha}{r-\mu_x}\theta_x + \frac{(1-\alpha)qc_0}{r-\mu_y}\theta_y + A\theta_x^{\gamma_2} & : & \theta_x > \bar{\theta}_x \wedge \theta_y > \bar{\theta}_y. \end{cases} \tag{A.38}$$

A.7 Determination of Coefficients - Arbitrary Change

Not demanding an optimal capability change - meaning that the capability value $\tilde{\theta}$ to apply the dynamic capability is externally given - the value matching condition is sufficient to determine the coefficient $\tilde{A}_2$ in the case of discarding capability x, and $\tilde{B}_1$ in the case of extending capability y. The result of $\tilde{A}_2$ is given by equation A.39, the result of $\tilde{B}_1$ by equation A.40:

$$\tilde{A}_2 = SV\tilde{\theta}_x^{-\gamma_2} - \frac{\alpha}{r-\mu_x}\tilde{\theta}_x^{1-\gamma_2} = \tilde{A} \tag{A.39}$$

$$\tilde{B}_1 = \frac{(q-1)c_0}{r-\mu_y}\tilde{\theta}_y^{1-\varepsilon_1} - qIC\tilde{\theta}_y^{-\varepsilon_1} = \tilde{B} \tag{A.40}$$

The firm value V_{Arb} in case of arbitrary capability change is given by equation A.41:

$$\tilde{V}(\theta_x, \theta_y) = \begin{cases} \frac{\alpha}{r-\mu_x}\theta_x + \frac{(1-\alpha)c_0}{r-\mu_y}\theta_y + \tilde{A}\theta_x^{\gamma_2} + \tilde{B}\theta_y^{\varepsilon_1} & : & \theta_x > \tilde{\theta}_x \wedge \theta_y < \tilde{\theta}_y \\[2ex] \frac{c_0}{r-\mu_y}\theta_y + \tilde{B}\theta_y^{\varepsilon_1} & : & \theta_x < \tilde{\theta}_x \wedge \theta_y < \tilde{\theta}_y \\[2ex] \frac{qc_0}{r-\mu_y}\theta_y & : & \theta_x < \tilde{\theta}_x \wedge \theta_y > \tilde{\theta}_y \\[2ex] \frac{\alpha}{r-\mu_x}\theta_x + \frac{(1-\alpha)qc_0}{r-\mu_y}\theta_y + \tilde{A}\theta_x^{\gamma_2} & : & \theta_x > \tilde{\theta}_x \wedge \theta_y > \tilde{\theta}_y. \end{cases} \tag{A.41}$$

Appendix B

Calculation of the Maximal Expected Cash Flow

B.1 Derivation of the PDE I

Examining the ambidextrous behavior of firms with regard to time and risk issues, it is sufficient to outline a model consisting of one firm operating in a declining market x with the option to withdraw from this market, and additionally possessing the option to enter an emerging market y.

Since both market developments are exogenously given and only partly predictable, a geometric Brownian Motion fulfills the made assumptions. The absolute cash flow changes $d\theta_x(t)$ and $d\theta_y(t)$ are described by equation B.1:

$$d\theta_x(t) = \mu_x\theta_x(t)dt + \sigma_x\theta_x(t)dW_x(t) \qquad \text{(B.1)}$$

$$d\theta_y(t) = \mu_y\theta_y(t)dt + \sigma_y\theta_y(t)dW_y(t).$$

The abandonment stage of market x is considered by an expected negative cash flow development $\mu_x < 0$. To ensure the solvability of the model the expected market development μ_y of the emerging market is given by $\mu_y \in [0, r[$, whereas r describes the risk less interest rate. Furthermore, I assume a correlation of the Wiener processes $dW_i \sim N(0,1)$, $(i = x, y)$ given by $E(dW_x dW_y) = \rho$.

The firm strives to maximize the over time accumulated cash flow and faces the decision problem described by equation B.2

$$
\begin{aligned}
V(\theta_x, \theta_y) \;=\; & \max_{\tau_1, \tau_2} E \left\{ \int_0^{\tau_1} c_x \theta_x e^{-rt} dt + \int_{\tau_1}^{\tau_2} \left[c_x \theta_x + c_y \theta_y \right] e^{-r(t-\tau_1)} dt + \int_{\tau_2}^{\infty} c_y \theta_y e^{-r(t-\tau_2)} dt \right\} \\
& - \; ICe^{-\tau_1 r} + SVe^{-\tau_2 r}.
\end{aligned}
\tag{B.2}
$$

With c_x and c_y I am able to control the intensity of the firm's commitment to exploit the markets x and y. In this context, I have to stress that the firm accepts only those salvage values (SV) and investment costs (IC), so that the introduction of the new product comes first, followed by the product withdrawal from the declining market.

The continuation value of equation B.2 is given by equation B.3:

$$
rV(\theta_x, \theta_y)dt = c_x \theta_x dt + E(dV).
\tag{B.3}
$$

$E(dV)$ describes the expected values consisting of the option value to exit market x and the option value to enter market y.

Since $V(\theta_x, \theta_y)$ depends on two diffusion processes, I have to apply the "two-dimensional" Itô's Lemma to specify dV from equation B.3:

$$
dV \;=\; \frac{\partial V}{\partial \theta_x} d\theta_x + \frac{\partial V}{\partial \theta_y} d\theta_y
$$
$$
+\; \frac{1}{2}\frac{\partial^2 V}{\partial \theta_x^2}(d\theta_x)^2 + \frac{1}{2}\frac{\partial^2 V}{\partial \theta_y^2}(d\theta_y)^2
$$
$$
+\; \frac{\partial^2 V}{\partial \theta_x \partial \theta_y} d\theta_x d\theta_y . \tag{B.4}
$$

With $(d\theta_x)^2 = \sigma_x^2 \theta_x^2 dt$, $(d\theta_y)^2 = \sigma_y^2 \theta_y^2 dt$, $d\theta_x d\theta_y = \rho \sigma_x \theta_x \sigma_y \theta_y dt$, I obtain the following differential equation:

$$
dV \;=\; \frac{\partial V}{\partial \theta_x} d\theta_x + \frac{\partial V}{\partial \theta_y} d\theta_y
$$
$$
+\; \frac{1}{2}\sigma_x^2 \theta_x^2 \frac{\partial^2 V}{\partial \theta_x^2} dt + \frac{1}{2}\sigma_y^2 \theta_y^2 \frac{\partial^2 V}{\partial \theta_y^2} dt
$$
$$
+\; \rho \sigma_x \sigma_y \theta_x \theta_y \frac{\partial^2 V}{\partial \theta_x \partial \theta_y} dt . \tag{B.5}
$$

Consequently the expectation value $E\{dV\}$ is given by:

$$
E\{dV\} \;=\; \mu_x \theta_x \frac{\partial V}{\partial \theta_x} dt + \mu_y \theta_y \frac{\partial V}{\partial \theta_y} dt
$$
$$
+\; \frac{1}{2}\sigma_x^2 \theta_x^2 \frac{\partial^2 V}{\partial \theta_x^2} dt + \frac{1}{2}\sigma_y^2 \theta_y^2 \frac{\partial^2 V}{\partial \theta_y^2} dt
$$
$$
+\; \rho \sigma_x \sigma_y \theta_x \theta_y \frac{\partial^2 V}{\partial x \partial y} dt , \tag{B.6}
$$

which leads me to the following differential equation:

$$
0 \;=\; -rV + c_x \theta_x + \mu_x \theta_x \frac{\partial V}{\partial \theta_x} + \mu_y \theta_y \frac{\partial V}{\partial \theta_y}
$$
$$
+\; \frac{1}{2}\sigma_x^2 \theta_x^2 \frac{\partial^2 V}{\partial \theta_x^2} + \frac{1}{2}\sigma_y^2 \theta_y^2 \frac{\partial^2 V}{\partial \theta_y^2} + \rho \sigma_x \sigma_y \theta_x \theta_y \frac{\partial^2 V}{\partial \theta_x \partial \theta_y} . \tag{B.7}
$$

The solution of this partial differential equation consists of a particulate solution and of a general solution of the homogeneous part of the differential equation.

B.2   Particulate Solution of the PDE I

The approach $V_p(\theta_x, \theta_y) = a\theta_x$ delivers with $a = \frac{c_x}{r-\mu_x}$ a possible solution:

$$V_p(\theta_x, \theta_y) = \frac{c_x}{r - \mu_x}\theta_x. \tag{B.8}$$

B.3   General Solution of the Homogeneous Part of the PDE I

The homogeneous part of the differential equation is expressed by:

$$
\begin{aligned}
0 \;=\; & \mu_x\theta_x\frac{\partial V}{\partial \theta_x} + \mu_y\theta_y\frac{\partial V}{\partial \theta_y} \\
+ \;& \frac{1}{2}\sigma_x^2\theta_x^2\frac{\partial^2 V}{\partial \theta_x^2} + \frac{1}{2}\sigma_y^2\theta_y^2\frac{\partial^2 V}{\partial \theta_y^2} \\
+ \;& \rho\sigma_x\sigma_y\theta_x\theta_y\frac{\partial^2 V}{\partial \theta_x\partial \theta_y} - rV.
\end{aligned}
\tag{B.9}
$$

A possible solution may be expressed as follows:

$$V_h(\theta_x, \theta_y) = A\theta_x^\gamma + B\theta_y^\varepsilon. \tag{B.10}$$

Considering $V_h(\theta_x, \theta_y)$ and the required derivations leads me to equation B.11:

$$
\begin{aligned}
0 &= -rA\theta_x^\gamma - rB\theta_y^\varepsilon + A\gamma\mu_x\theta_x^\gamma + B\varepsilon\mu_y\theta_y^\varepsilon \\[2mm]
&+ \frac{1}{2}\gamma(\gamma-1)A\sigma_x^2\theta_x^\gamma + \frac{1}{2}\varepsilon(\varepsilon-1)B\sigma_y^2\theta_y^\varepsilon \\[2mm]
&= A\theta_x^\gamma\left[-r + \gamma\mu_x + \frac{1}{2}\gamma(\gamma-1)\sigma_x^2\right] \\[2mm]
&+ B\theta_y^\varepsilon\left[-r + \varepsilon\mu_y + \frac{1}{2}\varepsilon(\varepsilon-1)\sigma_y^2\right].
\end{aligned}
\tag{B.11}
$$

This equation is fulfilled by:

$$
\gamma_{1,2} = \frac{1}{2} - \frac{\mu_x}{\sigma_x^2} \pm \sqrt{\left(\frac{1}{2} - \frac{\mu_x}{\sigma_x^2}\right)^2 + \frac{2r}{\sigma_x^2}}
\tag{B.12}
$$

and

$$
\varepsilon_{1,2} = \frac{1}{2} - \frac{\mu_y}{\sigma_y^2} \pm \sqrt{\left(\frac{1}{2} - \frac{\mu_y}{\sigma_y^2}\right)^2 + \frac{2r}{\sigma_y^2}}.
\tag{B.13}
$$

Hence, the solution of the differential equation is:

$$
\begin{aligned}
V(\theta_x, \theta_y) &= V_p + V_h \\[2mm]
&= a\theta_x + A_1\theta_x^{\gamma_1} + A_2\theta_x^{\gamma_2} \\[2mm]
&+ B_1\theta_y^{\varepsilon_1} + B_2\theta_y^{\varepsilon_2} \\[2mm]
&= \frac{c_x}{r - \mu_x}\theta_x + A_1\theta_x^{\gamma_1} + A_2\theta_x^{\gamma_2} \\[2mm]
&+ B_1\theta_y^{\varepsilon_1} + B_2\theta_y^{\varepsilon_2}.
\end{aligned}
\tag{B.14}
$$

The first addend $\frac{c_x}{r-\mu_x}\theta_x$ of equation B.14 represents the value generated by the firm operating in market x. The remaining summands are possible descriptions of the option value to exit market x $(A_1\theta_x^{\gamma_1}, A_2\theta_x^{\gamma_2})$ and to enter the market y $(B_1\theta_y^{\varepsilon_1}, B_2\theta_y^{\varepsilon_2})$. I use the value matching and smooth pasting condition to determine A_1, A_2, B_1 and B_2. To do this, I identify the value the firm generates by operating in market y.

B.4   Derivation of the PDE II

Analogous to the procedure given by equations B.2 and B.3, an equivalent to the discounted accumulated value, generated by operating in market y, described by equation B.15 is given by equation B.16:

$$V(\theta_y) = E\left\{\int_{\tau_2}^{\infty} c_y \theta_y(t) e^{-r(t-\tau_2)} dt\right\} \tag{B.15}$$

$$rV dt = c_y \theta_y dt + E(dV) \tag{B.16}$$

Using Itô's lemma dV is expressed by B.17:

$$dV = \frac{\partial V}{\partial \theta_y} d\theta_y + \frac{1}{2}\frac{\partial^2 V}{\partial \theta_y^2}(d\theta_y)^2. \tag{B.17}$$

I obtain the differential equation B.18 by inserting the expectation value of dV in equation B.16:

$$0 = \theta_y + \mu_y \theta_y \frac{\partial V}{\partial \theta_y} + \frac{1}{2}(\sigma_y^2)\theta_y^2 \frac{\partial^2 V}{\partial \theta_y^2} - rV. \tag{B.18}$$

B.5   Solution of the PDE II

The approach $V = \theta_y^\lambda$ leads to the characteristic equation:

$$\lambda^2 + \left(\frac{2\mu_y}{\sigma_{y1}^2 + \sigma_{y2}^2} - 1\right)\lambda - \frac{2r}{\sigma_y^2} = 0. \tag{B.19}$$

Hence, $\lambda_{1,2}$ are:

$$\lambda_{1,2} = \frac{1}{2} - \frac{\mu_y}{\sigma_y^2} \pm \sqrt{\left(\frac{1}{2} - \frac{\mu_y}{\sigma_y^2}\right)^2 + \frac{2r}{\sigma_y^2}}. \tag{B.20}$$

Because the perturbation factor θ_y follows the form θ_y^α I use the approach $C(\ln \theta_y)^k \theta_y^\alpha$

with $k = 0$ ($\alpha \neq \lambda_{1,2}$) and $\alpha = 1$. Using this approach in equation B.18 results in

$$C = \frac{c_y}{r - \mu_y}. \tag{B.21}$$

Hence, the solution of the differential equation B.16 is:

$$V(\theta_y) = \frac{c_y}{r - \mu_y}\theta_y + C_1\theta_y^{\lambda_1} + C_2\theta_y^{\lambda_2}. \tag{B.22}$$

$\frac{c_1}{r-\mu_y}\theta_y$ represents the generated value by the capability y. $C_1\theta_y^{\lambda_1}$ and $C_2\theta_y^{\lambda_2}$ are used to

determine the value of further options. As long as I do not consider further options, C_1

and C_2 are 0.

B.6   Determination of Coefficients

To determine A_1, A_2, B_1 and B_2, which might be possible solutions to describe the options

to enter market y and to exit market y, and $\bar{\theta}_i$ which indicates the values of θ_i to achieve

value maximization, I use the value matching and smooth pasting condition ($i = x, y$):

$$
\begin{aligned}
V_{VM}^x(\bar{\theta}_x, \theta_y) &= SV &= \frac{c_x}{r-\mu_x}\bar{\theta}_x &+ A_{1,2}\bar{\theta}_x^{\gamma_{1,2}} &+ B_{1,2}\theta_y^{\varepsilon_{1,2}} \\
V_{SP}^x(\bar{\theta}_x, \theta_y) &= 0 &= \frac{c_x}{r-\mu_x} &+ \gamma_{1,2}A_{1,2}\bar{\theta}_x^{\gamma_{1,2}-1} & \\
V_{VM}^y(\theta_x, \bar{\theta}_y) &= \frac{c_y}{r-\mu_y}\bar{\theta}_y - IC &= A_{1,2}\theta_x^{\gamma_{1,2}} &+ B_{1,2}\bar{\theta}_y^{\varepsilon_{1,2}} & \\
V_{SP}^y(\theta_x, \bar{\theta}_y) &= \frac{c_y}{r-\mu_y} &= \varepsilon_{1,2}B_{1,2}\bar{\theta}_y^{\varepsilon_{1,2}-1}. &
\end{aligned}
\tag{B.23}
$$

These equations must be fulfilled for all $\theta_i \in \mathbf{R}^{\geq 0}$. Therefore, I can set $\theta_i = 0$. Taking the co-domains of $\gamma_{1,2}$ ($\gamma_1 > 1 \wedge \gamma_2 < 0$) into account, the value of A_1 and consequently the option value given by $A_1 \theta_x^{\gamma_1}$ is negative. However, a negative option value does not describe an economic solution. The same considerations of $\varepsilon_{1,2}$ ($\varepsilon_1 > 1 \wedge \varepsilon_2 < 0$) lead to the result that the value to enter market y is given by $B_1 \theta_y^{\varepsilon_1}$.

$$
\begin{aligned}
A_2 &= \frac{c_x \bar{\theta}_x}{\gamma(\mu_x - r)} \bar{\theta}_x^{-\gamma} &&= A \\[2mm]
\gamma_2 &= \frac{1}{2} - \frac{\mu_x}{\sigma_x^2} - \sqrt{\left(\frac{1}{2} - \frac{\mu_x}{\sigma_x^2}\right)^2 + \frac{2r}{\sigma_x^2}} &&= \gamma \\[2mm]
B_1 &= \frac{c_y \bar{\theta}_y}{\varepsilon(r - \mu_y)} \bar{\theta}_y^{-\varepsilon} &&= B \\[2mm]
\varepsilon_1 &= \frac{1}{2} - \frac{\mu_y}{\sigma_y^2} + \sqrt{\left(\frac{1}{2} - \frac{\mu_y}{\sigma_y^2}\right)^2 + \frac{2r}{\sigma_y^2}} &&= \varepsilon \\[2mm]
\bar{\theta}_x &= \frac{r - \mu_x}{c_x} \frac{\gamma}{\gamma - 1} SV \\[2mm]
\bar{\theta}_y &= \frac{\varepsilon}{\varepsilon - 1} \frac{r - \mu_y}{c_y} IC
\end{aligned}
\tag{B.24}
$$

As equation B.25 shows, the calculation of V depends on the values θ_x and θ_y. Thus, I can distinguish the three following cases:

$$
V(\theta_x, \theta_y) = \begin{cases}
\frac{c_x}{r - \mu_x} \theta_x + A\theta_x^\gamma + B\theta_y^\varepsilon & : \quad \theta_x > \bar{\theta}_x \wedge \theta_y < \bar{\theta}_y \\[3mm]
\frac{c_x}{r - \mu_x} \theta_x + \frac{c_y}{r - \mu_y} \theta_y + A\theta_x^\gamma & : \quad \theta_x > \bar{\theta}_x \wedge \theta_y > \bar{\theta}_y \\[3mm]
\frac{c_y}{r - \mu_y} \theta_y & : \quad \theta_x < \bar{\theta}_x \wedge \theta_y > \bar{\theta}_y.
\end{cases}
\tag{B.25}
$$

Bibliography

ADLER, P. S., GOLDOFTAS, B. & LEVINE, D. I. (1999), 'Flexibility versus efficiency? A case study of model changeovers in the Toyota production system', *Organization Science* **10**(1), 43–68.

ADNER, R. & HELFAT, C. E. (2003), 'Corporate effects and dynamic managerial capabilities', *Strategic Management Journal* **24**(10), 1011–1025.

AMBROSINI, V. & BOWMAN, C. (2009), 'What are dynamic capabilities and are they a useful construct in strategic management?', *International Journal of Management Reviews* **11**(1), 29–49.

AMIT, R. & SCHOEMAKER, P. J. H. (1993), 'Strategic assets and organizational rent', *Strategic Management Journal* **14**, 33–46.

AMRAM, M. & KULATILAKA, N. (1999), *Real options: Managing strategic investments in an uncertain world*, Boston, MA: Harvard Business School Press.

ARGYRIS, C. & SCHÖN, D. (1978), *Organizational learning: A theory of action perspective*, Reading, Mass.: Addison-Wesley.

ATUAHENE-GIMA, K. (2005), 'Resolving the capability-rigidity paradox in new product innovation', *Journal of Marketing* **69**(4), 61–83.

BARNEY, J. (1991), 'Firm resources and sustained competitive advantage', *Journal of Management* **17**(1), 99–120.

BARNEY, J. B. (1986), 'Strategic factor markets: Expectations, luck, and business strategy', *Management Science* **32**(10), 1231–1241.

BARRETO, I. (2010), 'Dynamic capabilities: A reivew of past research and an agenda for the future', *Journal of Management* **36**(1), 256–280.

BAUM, J. A. C., XIAO LI, S. & USHER, J. M. (2000), 'Making the next move: How experiential and vicarious learning shape the locations of chains' acquisitions', *Administrative Science Quarterly* **45**(4), 766 – 801.

BENNER, M. J. & TUSHMAN, M. L. (2002), 'Process management and technological innovation: A longitudinal study of the photography and paint industries', *Administrative Science Quarterly* **47**(4), 676–706.

BENNER, M. J. & TUSHMAN, M. L. (2003), 'Exploitation, exploration, and process management: The productivity dilemma revisited', *Academy of Management Review* **28**(2), 238–256.

BIRKINSHAW, J. & GIBSON, C. (2004), 'Building ambidexterity into an organization', *MIT Sloan Management Review* **45**(4), 47–55.

BLYLER, M. & COFF, R. W. (2003), 'Dynamic capabilities, social capital, and rent appropriation: Ties that split pies', *Strategic Management Journal* **24**(7), 677–686.

BOWMAN, E. H. & HURRY, D. (1993), 'Strategy through the Option Lens: An Integrated View of Resource Investments and the Incremental-Choice Process', *Academy of Management Review* **18**(4), 760–782.

BOWMAN, E. H. & MOSKOWITZ, G. (2001), 'Real options analysis and strategic decision making', *Organization Science* **12**(6), 772–777.

BROWN, J. S. & DUGUID, P. (2001), 'Knowledge and organisation: A social-practice perspective.', *Organization Science* **12**(2), 198–213.

BURGELMAN, R. A. (1991), 'Intraorganizational ecology of strategy making and organizational adaptation: Theory and filed research', *Organization Science* **2**(3), 239–262.

BURGELMAN, R. A. (2002), 'Strategy as vector and the inertia of coevolutionary lock-in', *Administrative Science Quarterly* **47**(2), 325–357.

CHILDS, P. D. & TRIANTIS, A. J. (1999), 'Dynamic R&D investement policies', *Managment Science* **45**(10), 1359–1377.

COHEN, W. M. & LEVINTHAL, D. A. (1990), 'Absorptive capacity: A new perspective on learning and innovation', *Administrative Science Quarterly* **35**(1), 128–152.

CROWTHER, J., Hg. (1995), *Oxford Advanced Learner' Dictionary*, Oxford University Press.

DANNEELS, E. (2000), 'The dynamics of product innovation and firm competences', *Academy of Management Proceedings* **23**, D1–D6.

DANNEELS, E. (2002), 'The dynamics of product innovation and firm competences', *Strategic Management Journal* **23**(12), 1095–1121.

DEVAN, J., MILLAN, A. & SHIRKE, P. (2005), 'Balancing short- and long-term performance', *McKinsey Quarterly* **1**, 31–33.

DIERICKX, I. & COOL, K. (1989), 'Asset stock accumulation and sustainability of competitive advantage', *Management Science* **35**(12), 1504–1511.

DIXIT, A. K. (1992), 'Investment and hysteresis', *Journal of Economic Perspectives* **6**(1), 107–132.

DIXIT, A. K. & PINDYCK, R. S. (1994), *Investment under uncertainty*, Princeton, NJ: Princeton University Press.

DOUGHERTY, D. & HARDY, C. (1996), 'Sustained product innovation in large, mature organizations: Overcoming innovation-to-organization problems', *Academy of Management Journal* **39**(5), 1120 – 1153.

DUNCAN, R. B. (1976), The ambidexteritrous organisation: Designing dual structures for innovation, *in* N. Y. N. HOLLAND, Hg., 'The management of organisation design: Strategies and implementation', Kilmann R. H. and Pondy, L. R. and Slevin, D., Kap. The ambidextrous organization: Designing dual structures for innovation, S. 167–188.

EBBEN, J. J. & JOHNSON, A. C. (2005), 'Efficiency, flexibility, or both? Evidence linking strategy to performance in small firms', *Strategic Management Journal* **26**(13), 1249–1259.

EISENHARDT, K. M. & MARTIN, J. A. (2000), 'Dynamic capabilities: What are they?', *Strategic Management Journal* **21**(10/11), 1105–1121.

ETHIRAJ, S. K., KALE, P., KRISHNAN, M. S. & SINGH, J. V. (2005), 'Where do capabilities come from and how do they matter? A study in the software services industry', *Strategic Management Journal* **26**(1), 25–45.

FELDMAN, M. S. & PENTLAND, B. T. (2003), 'Reconceptualizing organisational routines as a source of flexbility and change', *Administrative Science Quarterly* **48**(1), 94–118.

GIBSON, C. B. & BIRKINSHAW, J. (2004), 'The antecedents, consequences, and mediating role of organizational ambidexterity', *Academy of Management Journal* **47**(2), 209–226.

GILBERT, C. (2005), 'Unbundling the structure of inertia: Ressource versus routine rigidity', *Academy of Management Journal* **48**(5), 741–763.

GILBERT, C. G. (2006), 'Change in the presence of residual fit: Can competing frames coexist?', *Organization Science* **17**(1), 150–167.

GRANT, R. M. (1996), 'Prospering in dynamically-competitive environments: Organizational capability as knowledge integration', *Organization Science* **7**(4), 375–387.

GRIFFITH, D. A. & HARVEY, M. G. (2001), 'A resource perspective of global dynamic capabilities', *Journal of International Business Studies* **32**(3), 597–606.

GUPTA, A. K., SMITH, K. G. & SHALLEY, C. E. (2006), 'The interplay between exploration and exploitation', *Academy of Management Journal* **49**(4), 693–706.

HANNAN, M. T. & FREEMAN, J. (1984), 'Structural inertia and organizational change', *American Sociological Review* **49**(2), 149–164.

HARRELD, J. B., O'REILLY, C. I. & TUSHMAN, M. L. (2007), 'Dynamic dapabilities at IBM: Driving strategy into action', *California Management Review* **49**(4), 21–43.

HELFAT, C. E. (1997), 'Know-how and Asset Complementarity and Dynamic Capability Accumulation: The Case of R&D', *Strategic Management Journal* **18**(5), 339–360.

HELFAT, C. E. & PETERAF, M. A. (2003), 'The dynamic resource-based view: Capability lifecycles', *Strategic Management Journal* **24**(10), 997–1010.

HELFAT, C. E. & RAUBITSCHEK, R. S. (2000), 'Product sequencing: Co-evolution of knowledge, capabilities and products', *Strategic Management Journal* **21**(10/11), 961–979.

HELFAT, C. E., FINKELSTEIN, S., MITCHELL, W., PETERAF, M. A., SINGH, H., TEECE, D. J. & WINTER, S. G. (2007), *Dynamic capabilities: understanding strategic change in organizations*, Malden, MA: Blackwell Publishing Ltd.

HENDERSON, R. & COCKBURN, I. (1994), 'Measuring competence? Exploring firm effects in pharmaceutical research', *Strategic Management Journal* **15**(Special Issue), 63–84.

HENDERSON, R. M. & CLARK, K. B. (1990), 'Architectural innovation: The reconfiguration of existing product technologies and the failure of established firms', *Administrative Science Quarterly* **35**(1), 9–30.

HE, Z.-L. & WONG, P.-K. (2004), 'Exploration vs. exploitation: An empirical test of the ambidexterity hypothesis', *Organization Science* **15**(4), 481–494.

HURLEY, R. F. & HULT, G. T. M. (1998), 'Innovation, market orientation, and organizational learning: An integration and empirical examination', *Journal of Marketing* **62**(3), 42–54.

HURRY, D. (1993), 'Restructuring in the gobal economy: The consequences of strategic linkages between Japanese and U.S. firms', *Strategic Management Journal* **14**(Special Issue), 69–82.

HURRY, D., MILLER, A. T. & BOWMAN, E. H. (1992), 'Calls on high-technology: Japanese exploration of venture capital investements in the United States', *Strategic Management Journal* **13**(2), 85–101.

IANSITI, M. & CLARK, K. (1994), 'Integration and dynamic capability: Evidence from product development in automobiles and mainframe computers', *Industrial and Corporate Change* **3**(3), 557–605.

JANSEN, J. J. P., VAN DEN BOSCH, F. A. J. & VOLBERDA, H. W. (2005), 'Exploratory innovation, exploitative innovation, and ambidexterity: The impact of environmental and organizational antecedents', *Schmalenbach Business Review (SBR)* **57**(4), 351–363.

JARZABKOWSKI, P. (2004), 'Strategy as a practice: Recursivenss, adaptation, and practices-in-use', *Organization Studies* **25**(4), 529–560.

KATILA, R. & AHUJA, G. (2002), 'Something old, something new: A longitudinal study of search and behavior and new product innovation', *Academy of Management Journal* **45**(6), 1183–1194.

KATKALO, V., PITELIS, C. & TEECE, D. (2010), 'Introduction: On the nature and scope of dynamic capabilities', *Industiral and Corporate Change* **19**(4), 1175–1186.

KAY, N. (2010), 'Dynamic capabilities as context: The role of decision, system and structure', *Industiral and Corporate Change* **19**(4), 1205–1223.

KELLY, G. A. (1955), *The psychology of personal constructs*, W. W. Norton & Company Inc., New York.

KESTER, W. C. (1984), 'Today's options for tomorrow's growth', *Harvard Business Review* **62**(2), 153–160.

KING, A. A. & TUCCI, C. L. (2002), 'Incumbent entry into new market niches: The role of experience and managerial choice in the creation of dynamic capabilities', *Management Science* **48**(2), 171–186.

KOGUT, B. (1991), 'Joint ventures and the option to expand and acquire', *Management Science* **37**(1), 19–33.

KOGUT, B. & KULATILAKA, N. (1994), 'Options thinking and platform investments: Investing in opportunity', *California Management Review* **36**(2), 52–71.

KOGUT, B. & KULATILAKA, N. (2001), 'Capabilities as real options', *Organization Science* **12**(6), 744–758.

KOGUT, B. & KULATILAKA, N. (2004), 'Real option pricing and organizations: The contingent risks of extended theoretical domains', *Academy of Management Review* **29**(1), 102–110.

KOGUT, B. & ZANDER, U. (1992), 'Knowledge of the firm, combinative capabilities, and the replication of technology', *Organization Science* **3**(3), 383–397.

KYLÄHEIKO, K., SANDSTRÖM, J. & VIRKKUNEN, V. (2002), 'Dynamic capability view in terms of real options', *International Journal of Production Economics* **80**(1), 65–83.

KYRIAKOPOULOS, K. & MOORMAN, C. (2004), 'Tradeoffs in marketing exploitation and exploration strategies: The overlooked role of market orientation', *International Journal of Research in Marketing* **21**(3), 219–240.

LAVIE, D. (2006), 'Capability reconfiguration: An analysis of incumbent responses to technological change', *Academy of Management Review* **31**(1), 153–174.

LAVIE, D. & ROSENKOPF, L. (2006), 'Balancing exploration and exploitation in alliance formation', *Academy of Management Journal* **49**(4), 797–818.

LEE, J., LEE, J. & LEE, H. (2003), 'Exploration and exploitation in the presence of network externalities', *Management Science* **49**(4), 553–570.

LEE, J., LEE, K. & RHO, S. (2002), 'An evolutionary perspective on strategic group emergence: A genetic algorithm-based model', *Strategic Management Journal* **23**(8), 727–746.

LEVINTHAL, D. A. & MARCH, J. G. (1993), 'The myopia of learning', *Strategic Management Journal* **14**(Special Issue), 95–112.

LEVITT, B. & MARCH, J. G. (1988), 'Organizational learning', *Annual Review of Sociology* **14**(1), 319–340.

MAKADOK, R. (2001), 'Toward a synthesis of the resource-based and dynamic capability views of rent creation', *Strategic Management Journal* **22**(5), 387–401.

MALONE, T. & CROWSTON, K. (1994), 'The interdisciplinary study of coordination', *ACM Computing Surveys* **26**(1), 87–119.

MARCH, J. G. (1991), 'Exploration and exploitation in organizational learning', *Organization Science* **2**(1), 71–86.

MARCH, J. G. (2006), 'Rationality, foolishness, and adaptive intelligence', *Strategic Management Journal* **27**(3), 201–214.

MARKIDES, C. & CHARITOU, C. D. (2004), 'Competing with dual business models: A contingency approach', *Academy of Management Executive* **18**(3), 22–36.

MARSH, S. J. & STOCK, G. N. (2006), 'Creating dynamic capability: The role of intertemporal integration, knowledge retention, and interpretation', *The Journal of Product Innovation Management* **23**(5), 422–436.

MCGRATH, R. G. (1997), 'A real options logic for initiationg technology positioning investements', *Academy of Management Review* **22**(4), 974–996.

MENGUC, B. & AUH, S. (2006), 'Creating a firm-level dynamic capabilitiy through capitalzing on market orientation and innovativenes', *Academy of Marketing Science* **34**(1), 63–73.

NELSON, R. R. (1991), 'Why do firms differ, and how does it matter?', *Strategic Management Journal* **12**(Special Issue), 61–74.

NELSON, R. R. & WINTER, S. G. (1982), *An evolutionary theory of economic change*, Cambridge, Mass.: Harvard University Press.

NI, N. & WAN, F. (2008), 'A configurational perspective of branding capabilities development in emerging economies: The case of the chines cellular phone industry', *Journal of Brand Management* **15**(6), 433–451.

O'REILLY, C. A. & TUSHMAN, M. L. (2004), 'The ambidextrous organization', *Harvard Business Review* **82**(4), 74–81.

O'REILLY, C. A. & TUSHMAN, M. L. (2007), 'Ambidexterity as a dynamic capability: Resolving the innovator's dilemma', *Harvard Business School Working Paper*.

PABLO, A., R., T., DEWALD, J. & CASEBEER, A. (2007), 'Identifying, enabling and managing dynamic capabilities in the public sector.', *Journal of Management Studies* **44**(5), 687–708.

PETERAF, M. A. (1993), 'The cornerstones of competitive advantage: A resource-based view', *Strategic Management Journal* **14**(3), 179–191.

PORTER, M. E. (1980*a*), *Competitive strategy*, NY: Free Press.

PORTER, M. E. (1980*b*), 'How competitive forces shape strategy', *McKinsey Quarterly* **2**(2), 34–50.

PROBST, G. & RAISCH, S. (2005), 'Organizational crisis: The logic of failure', *Academy of Management Executive* **19**(1), 90 – 105.

RAISCH, S. & BIRKINSHAW, J. (2008), 'Organizational ambidexterity: Antecedents, outcomes, and moderators.', *Journal of Management* **34**(3), 375–409.

ROSENBLOOM, R. S. (2000), 'Leadership, capabilities, and technological change: The transformation of NCR in the electronic era', *Strategic Management Journal* **21**, 1083–1104.

SCHREYÖGG, G. & KLIESCH-EBERL, M. (2007), 'How dynamic can organizational capabilities be? Towards a dual-process model of capability dynamization', *Strategic Management Journal* **28**(9), 913–933.

SCHUMPETER, J. A. (1934), *The theory of economic development*, Harvard University Press: Cambridge, MA., 7th edn (transl. Opie R).

SHAPIRO, C. (1989), 'The theory of business strategy', *RAND Journal of Economics* **20**(1), 125–137.

SIGGELKOW, N. & LEVINTHAL, D. A. (2003), 'Temporarily divide to conquer: Centralized, decentralized, and reintegrated organizational approaches to exploration and adaptation', *Organization Science* **14**(6), 650–669.

SIGGELKOW, N. & RIVKIN, J. W. (2006), 'When exploration backfires: Unintended consequences of multilevel organizational search', *Academy of Management Journal* **49**(4), 779–795.

SITKIN, B. S., SUTCLIFFE, K. M. & SCHROEDER, R. G. (1994), 'Distinguishing control from learning in Total Quality Management: A contingency perspective', *Academy of Management Review* **19**(3), 537–564.

SLATER, S. F. & NARVER, J. C. (1995), 'Market orientation and the learning organization.', *Journal of Marketing* **59**(3), 63–74.

SMITH, W. K. & TUSHMAN, M. L. (2005), 'Managing strategic contradictions: A top management model for managing innovation streams', *Organization Science* **16**(5), 522–536.

SONG, J. (2001), Modelling rteal option: A first passage time approach, Technischer bericht, Napier University Business School, Edinburgh EH11 4BN, UK.

STEFANO, G., PETERAF, M. & VERONA, G. (2010), 'Dynamic capabilities deconstructed: Bibliographic investigation into the origins, development and future directions of research domain', *Industiral and Corporate Change* **19**(4), 1187–1204.

TEECE, D. J. (2007), 'Explicating dynamic capabilities: The nature and microfoundations of (sustainable) enterprise performance', *Strategic Management Journal* **28**(13), 1319–1350.

TEECE, D. J. & PISANO, G. (1994), 'The dynamic capabilities of firms: An introduction', *Industiral and Corporate Change* **3**(3), 537–556.

TEECE, D. J., PISANO, G. & SHUEN, A. (1997), 'Dynamic capabilities and strategic management', *Strategic Management Journal* **18**(7), 509–533.

TRIGEORGIS, L. (1993), 'The nature of option interactions and the valuation of investments with multiple real options', *Journal of Financial and Quantitative Analysis* **28**(1), 1–20.

TUSHMAN, M. L. & O'REILLY, C. A. (1996), 'Ambidextrous organizations: Managing evolutionary and revolutionary change', *California Management Review* **38**(4), 8–30.

TUSHMAN, M. L. & ROMANELLI, E. (1985), 'Organizational evolution: A metamorphosis model of convergence and reorientation.', *Research in Organizational Behavior* **7**(11), 171–222.

UHLENBRUCK, K., MEYER, K. E. & HITT, M. A. (2003), 'Organisational transformation in transition economies: Resource-based and organisational learning perspectives', *Journal of Management Studies* **40**(2), 179–211.

VAN DEN BOSCH, F. A., VOLBERDA, H. W. & DE BOER, M. (1999), 'Coevolution of firm absorptive capacity and knowledge environment: organizational forms and combinative capabilities', *Organization Science* **10**(5), 551–568.

VASSOLO, R. S., ANAND, J. & FOLTA, T. B. (2004), 'Non-additivity in portfolios of exploration activities: A real options-based analysis of equity alliances in biotechnology', *Strategic Management Journal* **25**, 1045–1061.

VERMEULEN, F. & BARKEMA, H. (2001), 'Learning through acquisitions.', *Academy of Management Journal* **44**(3), 457 – 476.

VOLBERDA, H. W. (1996), 'Toward the flexible form: How to remain vital in hypercompetitive environments', *Organization Science* **7**(4), 359–374.

WANG, C. L. & AHMED, P. K. (2007), 'Dynamic capabilities: A review and research agenda', *International Journal of Management Reviews* **9**(1), 31–55.

WEBSTER, J. & WATSON, R. T. (2002), 'Analyzing the past to prepare for the future: Writing a literature review', *MIS Quarterly* **26**(2), 13–23.

WEICK, K. E. & ROBERTS, K. H. (1993), 'Collective mind in organizations: Heedful interrelating on flight decks', *Administrative Science Quarterly* **38**(3), 357–381.

WILLIAMSON, O. E. (1991), 'Comparative economic organization: The analysis of discrete structural alternatives', *Administrative Science Quarterly* **36**(2), 269–296.

WINTER, S. G. (2003), 'Understanding dynamic capabilities', *Strategic Management Journal* **24**(10), 991–995.

ZAHRA, S. A., SAPIENZA, H. J. & DAVIDSSON, P. (2006), 'Entrepreneurship and dynamic capabilities: A review, model and research agenda', *Journal of Management Studies* **43**(4), 917–955.

ZANDER, U. & KOGUT, B. (1995), 'Knowledge and the speed of the transfer and imitation of organizational oapabilities: An empirical test', *Organization Science* **6**(1), 76–92.

ZOLLO, M. & WINTER, S. G. (2002), 'Deliberate learning and the evolution of dynamic capabilities', *Organization Science* **13**(3), 339–351.

ZOTT, C. (2003), 'Dynamic capabilities and the emergence of intraindustry differential firm performance: Insights from a simulation study', *Strategic Management Journal* **24**(2), 97–125.